BEST
INTENTIONS

BEST
INTENTIONS

ENSURING YOUR ESTATE PLAN
DELIVERS BOTH WEALTH AND WISDOM

Colleen Barney, Esq.

Victoria Collins, Ph.D., CFP

Dearborn™
Trade Publishing
A **Kaplan Professional** Company

Editorial Director: Donald J. Hull
Senior Managing Editor: Jack Kiburz
Interior Design: Lucy Jenkins
Cover Design: Design Solutions
Typesetting: Elizabeth Pitts

Printed in the United States of America

02 03 04 10 9 8 7 6 5 4 3 2 1

Library of Congress Cataloging-in-Publication Data

Barney, Colleen.
   Best intentions : ensuring your estate plan delivers both wealth and
wisdom / Colleen Barney, Victoria Collins.
       p.   cm.
     ISBN 0-7931-5196-1 (hard)
     1. Estate planning—United States—Popular works.   I. Collins,
Victoria F. (Victoria Felton), 1942–   II. Title.
   KF750.Z9 B365 2002
   346.7305'2—dc21

                                                              2001007520

Dedication

This book is dedicated . . .

To our clients who shared their personal stories

To our families who show us daily the importance of knowing our values

And to the victims of the terrorist attacks who never had a chance to say good-bye

FOREWORD

So many books focus on how to create wealth when we are young, accumulate more wealth as we grow older, and pass on that wealth to our families when we die. With all of this focus on wealth, we can easily lose sight of other important things. The fact is that no matter how much wealth we accumulate, we still need to have the foresight to pass along our values and ideals to our loved ones. What good is our money if we are not responsible with it? What have we really given our children if we have not taught them to handle their financial resources responsibly?

The book you are holding is the result of lessons and insights that my coauthor, Colleen Barney, and I began to discover in our practices. Clients and colleagues shared their stories of best-laid plans that didn't work out the way they had intended. In most cases, it wasn't a lack of planning or procrastination that was the culprit. Indeed, in some cases, elaborate estate plans were made only to find out later that the players central to the plans didn't get along. We noticed that it is a lot easier to make plans about how to pass on the tangible parts of our lives—stocks, bonds, cash, and property—than it is to pass on the intangible values of hopes and dreams.

Although Colleen and I come from two different professions—estate planning versus financial planning and investment management—the common thread is that we both help clients express their needs and goals and then work with them to accomplish what they want. I like to think of my work as helping clients meet goals during life, while Colleen's is about ensuring those and other goals continue to be met after life.

A driving force for this book were the stories we heard from clients and colleagues about the best intentions people have for what they want (or don't want) for their heirs, and then what really happens. We knew we had to somehow capture those stories and "tease out" the patterns and the lessons. It was challenging but enjoyable. We shared many a lunch listening to CPAs, financial advisors, clients, and others recount their stories. The pages of the book began to fill with heartwarming, often poignant, sometimes sad, but always captivating stories of real people facing real situations.

During the process of writing, which Colleen shouldered to a great extent, we shared our own stories from different stages in our lives. We bring the different perspectives of age, but we were struck by a strong common denominator: Colleen is passionate about what she wants to share with her two young daughters, Julia and Rachel. I feel equally passionate about my eight grandchildren: Morgan, David, Alex, Derek, Timothy, Audrey, Daniel, and Liam. I want them to be financially responsible, to make family and friends a priority, and to value their education and their country. I also want them to be considerate and sensitive to others and to help those who are less fortunate. For me, philanthropy is important, and I'd like them to have an interest no matter what their level of wealth turns out to be. As you read this book, you'll find many examples of how estate planning can ensure such values get passed on.

One of the things my husband David and I always tried to instill in our five children was that they needed to make their way in this world without needing to rely on us. We were able to pass on to them the lessons of hard work, and they were able to take those lessons and learn from them. In this book, we've included many examples of how we could have instilled those values and taught those lessons even if we were not here to do it ourselves.

You'll also see several of our roles reflected in our writing: mother, grandmother, stepmother, wife, and busy professional. Sometimes, meeting the demands of our different roles feels like we're being pulled in several directions at the same time. Men are no strangers to this feeling, either. It's a lot tougher today to pass on values when children are bombarded with multiple and often mixed messages from parents who may be single, married, divorced, widowed, or remarried. Many children have a mother, father, stepmother, stepfather, siblings, and stepsiblings—no wonder there's confusion. It's hard enough to pass on values when we can model them day-by-day, but imagine estate planning in these complex situations.

I believe that now, even more than ever before, we in this country need to focus on what is really important to us. It is not the wealth we accumulate, but it is what we do with that wealth. It would be wonderful if we could take the time during our lives to pass on the lessons we have learned to our loved ones—lessons about being self-sufficient, responsible, thrifty, caring, and so many other values. Unfortunately, not everyone gets the chance to instill all the ideals they would like. Some people die early or unexpectedly. Some ignore the fact that death is inevitable. And some get so caught up in the tools and techniques of passing wealth that they forget about the wisdom they also have to share.

Best Intentions encourages us to look inside ourselves, to identify what is important to us, and to see our estate plan from the perspective of those who come after us. We hope this book prompts thoughtful reflection, meaningful dialogue, and estate planning that does just what you want it to do.

—Victoria Collins, Ph.D., CFP

CONTENTS

PREFACE

It's funny how we think about things. When we raise our families, we spend countless hours teaching our children all sorts of lessons. We subtly or sometimes not so subtly pass on to them our desires about college education and about being contributing members of society. We make sure that they understand we do not condone drug abuse or violence against others. Although the lessons may change, we continue to pass on the wisdom of age to our children even after they grow up. We give advice regarding careers and parenting. We talk to our children about the appropriateness of their choices for mates, lifestyles, and behaviors. Why do we stop at death? We are not talking about séances and other similar types of communication after death, but about the greatest legacy we can give our families: to continue passing the wisdom we have acquired through the last written documents we leave them—our estate plan.

Children are not our only concern when designing our estate plans. Some of us don't have children, and others of us have more than just our children to think about. Do we feel any less strongly that our nieces and nephews have a college education than our children? Not at all. Do we worry about giving something to one sibling and not to another? Of course. If we are providing for our parents while we are alive, would they no longer need the help just because we have died? Certainly not.

We know many clients, friends, and others who focus only on probate avoidance or estate tax reduction when preparing their estate plans. We would like to challenge them—and you—to think about what your estate plan says to your family. Does your estate plan pass on the wisdom and lessons you would if you were still here? How can you pass on your estate in a way that ensures you have provided more than just cash to your loved ones? How do you transfer your visions and ideals, values and morals, work ethic and guidance, and most important, your love?

In this book, you will find stories and letters from and about real people, people just like you who, despite their best intentions, did not pass on what they intended—their own special messages and lessons. This book will challenge you to develop special messages to pass to your loved ones and then find ways to communicate those messages even after your death.

Before you start reading this book, sit down and answer these three simple questions:

1. If you died today, do you still have lessons left to teach your loved ones?

2. If you could see what you left behind, what would cause you the greatest disappointment? The greatest pride? The greatest sense of accomplishment?

3. What unintended messages may be sent to your loved ones in your current plan? By your lack of a plan?

Once you have the answers to these questions, then read about others who, though having the best of intentions, didn't pass the life lessons they wanted.

This book will not explain how to avoid probate or minimize taxes. This book will not teach you when a QTIP trust is better than an A-B trust. This book will not tell you when a springing power of attorney is better than an immediate power of attorney. This book is about you and the most important lessons you want to pass on to others. It will help you make sure that your estate plan not only does what the law says it should do, but actually does what *you* want it to do. It will help you take your best intentions and make them a reality.

—Colleen Barney, Esq.

ACKNOWLEDGMENTS

This book could never have been written without the heartfelt stories from so many dear clients. They shared their hopes and dreams, fears and frustrations, in a sincere effort to pass both wealth and wisdom to those they care about. It is always a privilege and a pleasure to work with such clients.

Our professional friends and colleagues provided valuable input as we worked to gather relevant concepts and "tease out" the major themes. We especially thank Jeffrey Hipshman, Marilyn Millare, and Barbara Clark at HMWC, CPAs and Business Advisors in Tustin, California; and Darliene Evans at First American Trust Corporation in Santa Ana, California, who shared her extensive expertise in trusts and provided valuable insights for this book.

We thank our partners, Rick Albrecht at Albrecht & Barney, and Rick Keller, John Hakopian, and Marr Leisure at the Keller Group Investment Management, Inc., for their help and support while we were working on this book. Betty Jandete, proofreader *extraordinaire,* so graciously offered her time and talent and was a wonderful support all along the way.

Deep appreciation goes to our husbands and children, Jonathan Barney and daughters Rachel and Julia Barney, and David Collins. Our families have a special understanding for the time and energy it takes to write a book such as this, and we thank them for their never-failing support and encouragement.

We also would like to recognize and thank the following individuals: Robert Ormerod, Mary Jo Ormerod, John Lennon I, Florence Lennon, John Lennon II, Carrie Lennon, Maggie Lennon, Scott Sutphin, Kelly Sutphin, Stacey Sutphin, Kim Sutphin, Tiara Tatarczuk, Dan Lennon, Alex Jandete, Linda Coombs, Dorothy Galaz, Patricia Cusick, and Jennifer Millington.

1

Failing to Plan
Is Planning to Fail

JANINE'S STORY

When Bruce and I got married, we promised to love, honor, and cherish each other. We promised to take care of each other in sickness and in health. And even though we said 'til death do us part, I never really thought that our obligation to each other ended at death. I was barely 22 when we got married. Bruce was 28 and had been married once before. He had a three-year-old daughter from his first marriage. It wasn't until our son was born two years later that I started to think about our own mortality. I would get nervous every time we got on a plane. If something happened to us, what would happen to the children?

I started asking Bruce about doing a will. He would laugh and tell me that I was being silly. We were only in our 20s and early 30s, why would we possibly need a will? Sometimes the discussions would turn into fights, because I didn't feel he took my concerns seriously. He was a good father and a good husband in so many ways that I just couldn't understand why he was so stubborn on this point. Didn't he care what would happen to the children if something happened to us? The issue would come up around vacation time but would be forgotten throughout the rest of the year.

Then Aunt June died and we went to her funeral. Aunt June was 82 and had lived a good long life. During the service, the minister talked about the great life Aunt June had led. He told us she knew at the end that her time left on earth was short and that it was an incredible opportunity for her to tie up loose ends—to say her good-byes, to finish any unfinished business, and to show everyone the love she had for her family. Then he asked us to think about our lives and whether we had unfinished business to take care of. He told us that we may not all have the blessing that Aunt June had of knowing when her time was coming to an end. He reminded us that we could die that day, the next day, or the next week. He encouraged us to make sure that we showed our families how much we loved them by not leaving them with our unfinished business.

On the way home, I told Bruce that I thought the minister really made a good point about getting our affairs in order, because we never know when our time might come. Bruce laughed and said I was too emotional. We barely spoke the rest of the night.

The next day, Bruce's boss called me from work. There was an accident at the construction site, and Bruce was being flown to the nearest trauma hospital. I frantically raced to the hospital, but by the time I got there, Bruce had already died.

Before I even had time to make all of the funeral arrangements, I got a call from Denise, Bruce's ex-wife. She wanted to know what types of provisions Bruce had made for their daughter, Brianna. When I told her that

Bruce had not made any arrangements, she accused me of lying and told me that she was going to make sure that Brianna received her fair share of Bruce's estate. I kept thinking to myself, What estate? We had a nice home and a few dollars in the bank, but that was it. There was a $50,000 life insurance policy, but that would just barely help us pay off the mortgage and the burial expenses. I hoped Denise would calm down, so that we could talk about this rationally.

It has been four years since Bruce's death. Denise sued the estate claiming that almost everything Bruce and I had worked for together should go to Brianna. I love Brianna dearly and would have gladly made sure she was provided for, but I also needed to provide for our son and myself. I have had to borrow thousands of dollars from my parents to fight Denise and her lawyers. I have had to prove that there was no will, no trust, nothing indicating how Bruce wanted his estate to be divided. But how do you prove that a father of two, who seemed by all other indications to be a great dad, didn't make provisions for his children in the event of his death? I wonder how Bruce could have cared so little about all of us that he did not make any plans for us.

Showing That You Care

Sometimes saying nothing says a lot to others. The problem is that it probably doesn't say what you really mean. By failing to plan your estate, you cannot come back at a later date and tell your family and friends that you really did care. Failing to plan leaves those you love with the message that you really didn't care enough. You put thought into what you are going to wear each day, where to have lunch, what you will do over the weekend. Why not put some thought into what will happen if you do not have a tomorrow to fix things? Most people put more time and effort into planning their summer vacation than they do into how they are going to take care of their families after they die. Is that the message you want to pass on to your family—that a vacation was worth more of your attention than planning for them in their time of need?

Bruce easily could have prepared a short will indicating how his estate should be divided among Brianna, Janine, and their son. Instead, he did nothing. Given all of his other positive qualities, it is not likely that Bruce failed to plan his estate because he did not care about his family. As a man in his early 30s, he probably did not want to focus on his own mortality. Planning how to pay the bills day-to-day was likely of greater importance than planning for an event that he did not envision happening until much later in life.

Even if you are not married, do not have children, or are not a millionaire, you should consider preparing an estate plan. The purpose of your estate plan is to ensure that you can pass on the messages you want, to the people you care about, under the conditions that you dictate. Here is what happens if you do not have an estate plan:

- *The state decides who makes your medical decisions for you in the event you are unable.* Most people think of estate plans as documents that determine what happens after death. Actually, some of the most important estate planning dictates what happens while you are still alive. Health care directives, living wills, or durable powers of attorney for health care all allow you to name someone who can make medical decisions for you in the event you are unable. Powers of attorney for asset management allow you to name someone who can sign your name to financial documents. Living trusts can state the manner in which you want your finances handled, how distributions should be made to you and your family if you are no longer in a position to make those types of decisions, and who will be responsible for your affairs under certain circumstances.

- *The state decides who inherits your assets.* This could mean your spouse, your children, your parents, your siblings, or some more distant relative, depending on your circumstances. It is possible that you and the state think alike when it comes to naming your beneficiaries, but what are the chances of that? The rules are the same for every person in the state. Look at your neighbors next door, across the street, and around the corner. What is the likelihood that you will all have the same opinions on who should inherit your assets at death?

- *The state decides under what conditions your beneficiaries inherit your assets.* For young children, it is possible that a court would order the assets to stay in a trust until age 18, or maybe 21. Personally, I know that if my children get all of my money at age 18 or age 21, there will be a really nice Porsche purchased (and possibly wrecked) before age 19 or 22. If I am not willing to give my children all of my money at age 18 or 21 while I am alive, assuming there is some other way for me to survive, why on earth would I let someone else do it at my death when I am no longer here to give them guidance?

Knowing When to Ask for Help

Sometimes when we are driving in an unfamiliar area, I will turn to my husband and suggest that we stop and ask for directions. My husband will be the first to admit that he has the worst sense of direction of anyone we know. He still passes our exit on the freeway coming home from a night with friends. Yet, as soon as I make the suggestion to stop and ask, he sits up straighter in his seat and says with great confidence that he knows right where we are. Generally, it takes at least another half-hour before he breaks down and stops to ask for directions. I always think of my husband when I see people who do their estate plans by themselves. Somehow, they have convinced themselves that they do not need anyone else's help, that they can do this by themselves.

MICHAEL'S LETTER

Dear Steve,

When you married my mother, I could see how much she meant to you. It was the first time in a while that I felt Mom was going to be okay. She finally had someone to love her, to cherish her, and to provide for her. She deserved it. Over the years, I developed a great respect for you. I knew you would never do anything to hurt my mother. Imagine how surprised I was to find out just how much you did hurt her.

I know you didn't hurt her intentionally. And, I am sure you would have done things differently if you had known how things were going to turn out. So, let me tell you what has happened since you died.

I know you never liked lawyers, and frankly, I don't blame you. But because you refused to seek legal help during your life, we are now forced to seek legal help after your death. We have been forced to probate your estate. Do you know what probate is like? For starters, we couldn't access your bank accounts or cash any bonds, until the probate was formally started. That took six weeks, six weeks that the phone bill, the electric bill, the gas bill, and the water bill could not get paid. I didn't mind giving Mom the money, but if you could have seen the look on her face when she had to ask. I just know you couldn't have intended that.

One of the requirements to get the probate officially started was that I apply for a bond. I had to pay several thousand dollars out of my own pocket to qualify to serve as executor of your estate. I understand that, even if you had one of those cheap store-bought wills instead of writing one on the free notepads from your local Realtor, the bond requirement would have been waived. It is not that I mind the money. I just know that you couldn't have intended that.

Mom was in desperate need of some money once the probate had finally started. Because she was not the only beneficiary of your estate, I could not ask for a spousal allowance to be made without reducing your other beneficiaries' shares. I didn't think that would be fair. I tried to ask the judge to make an early distribution to Mom of just a small part of the estate. Unfortunately, this couldn't be done until two more months had passed. As soon as the two-month mark passed, I again made the request to the court. This time I was told that Mom would first have to be bonded (in case the court needed to ask for some of the money back). Because Mom didn't have any assets of her own, the bond was denied. I was then told that Mom could have an early distribution if I made another request in two more months. Finally, just over six months after you died, I got a small, early distribution to Mom. It was just enough to get her by. It is not that I am not thankful that you left Mom some of your estate, I am. I just know that you couldn't have intended that.

I thought it was such a nice gesture that you left your grandson some of your personal effects, especially since you and your son had never been very close. Because your grandson is under 18, however, we had to incur additional accounting and other expenses that generally could have been waived. This meant Mom got even less. I do not begrudge your grandson the bequest. I just know you couldn't have intended that.

You promised me, when you asked if you could marry my mother, that you would protect her. Thank you for keeping your promise throughout your marriage. I know my mother treasures the years you spent together. She felt loved and safe and that was because of you. When you died, though, you broke your promise. And, I just know you couldn't have intended that.

Yours sincerely,

Michael

You can see from Michael's letter that there is a real problem with not asking for help with your estate plan when you need it. It is an important part of the learning experience to admit you do not know everything and to ask for help when you need it. This is the positive message you send to your children by asking for help in preparing your estate plan.

Do you remember the day you came home with your first child? You would think that taking care of a newborn would be instinctive, but it was anything but instinctive, right? I do not think my children would have lived to see their first birthdays if my husband and I had not been willing to ask questions of our family, friends, neighbors, doctors, and frankly anyone who was willing to answer us. Most of us hope that our children will come to us when they become parents to ask for advice. But how can they trust us with their questions, if we don't teach them when and how to ask for advice?

EVELYN'S STORY

Mom and I were best friends. That is probably common between only children and their parents. We went through a lot together. Dad's illness was long, and his death was tough on both of us. We made a pact after Dad's death that we each would make sure the other was always taken care of in case something unforeseen happened.

We both set up living trusts that provided for each other in the event one of us died. The lawyer told us we needed to put all of our assets into the trusts, but Mom was never convinced the trust would be enough. I agreed with her. I knew Mom would be taken care of if I died, but what if I got sick? Would Mom be able to get into my bank accounts? Would she be able to take care of herself, or me, if necessary?

We decided to put our real estate into our trusts but to keep our cash in joint bank accounts. We had gone to plenty of seminars, so we knew that a joint tenancy bank account would not be probated if one of us died.

We were meticulous about accounting for our assets. For Mom's accounts, we added my name but continued to report the accounts under her Social Security number. We made sure that the rent she collected on her properties only went into her accounts. We did the same for my accounts. We were our accountant's dream clients.

When Mom died, the accountant had to prepare an estate tax return. I got him the date of death balances in each of Mom's accounts, appraisals for her real estate, and the value of the contents of her house. I was surprised when he asked for the balances in my bank accounts. He explained that because Mom's name was on my accounts, we had to report the accounts on her estate tax return.

We didn't have to pay estate tax on the accounts, he explained, we just had to report them.

My heart fell when I saw the return address from the IRS on the envelope in my mailbox. In the over 30 years I had been filing my taxes, I had never been audited. It took me several minutes to realize that it was my mother's estate, not my personal return, that was being audited. All of the questions from the auditor were about those joint bank accounts.

The IRS was trying to claim that I had to pay estate taxes on all of the money in my bank accounts just because my mother's name was on those accounts. The accounts totaled roughly $1,000,000, and the extra tax was almost $500,000. According to the IRS, the accounts were part of my mother's estate unless I could prove that the money was mine. I gave them copies of my income tax returns showing my reporting 100 percent of the interest income. They said that wasn't good enough. They wanted copies of all checks that had been deposited for the past five years. That way they could tell if any of the checks made out to Mom were deposited into my accounts.

The bank first told me that they could not provide that kind of information. Eventually, I convinced them that I wasn't going away until they gave me what the IRS was requesting. This process had to be repeated at each and every bank. It cost me several hundred dollars and many hours arguing with bank personnel, but eventually I got five years of microfiche copies of every check that had been deposited into my accounts.

Thank goodness we had been so careful about keeping track of our money separately. The IRS eventually conceded that the money in my accounts was actually my money, and I did not owe any additional estate tax on it. When I was going through the audit, our estate planning attorney asked me why we hadn't put the accounts into our separate trusts. I explained our concerns about access to the funds and our need to make sure the other was cared for properly. He told me that the trusts would have been able to do everything we wanted, and there would not have been an issue for the IRS. That is when it hit me. We never told the lawyer about our concerns or asked his advice on our plan. We had been to the seminars, we knew all there was to know, so why bother with the lawyer? I guess we weren't as smart as we thought we were.

Understanding Your Own Limitations

When you do your own estate plan without seeking advice from an authoritative source, you are teaching your loved ones that it is better to trust their own knowledge than to ask for professional help. It is only after you die that they learn the hard way to ask for advice when they need it.

You cannot do it by yourself. As much as it is hard to accept at times, there are good reasons why we have lawyers, who are trained to do things like drafting wills and trusts. That is not to say that all lawyers are competent in areas such as estate planning, but they are much more likely to know how to tell you how to get where you want to. Without getting professional help, you can easily be setting up your family for unintended problems. When you are in unfamiliar territory, you do not always know where the problem areas may be or how to avoid them. You need to rely on competent professionals to get you to your intended destination. However, remember that not all lawyers are competent professionals in the area of estate planning.

WENDY'S STORY

My parents were kind but unsophisticated people. They owned a tool and die shop. It didn't make them millions, but they did pretty well for themselves. As they started getting older, my brother and I talked to them endlessly about getting a will or a trust. We had heard too many stories from our friends about the horrors of dealing with the estates of parents who failed to do any planning. My parents were actually pretty open to the idea. At least, that is what I initially thought.

One weekend when both Terry and I were at their house, Dad and Mom showed us their wills. They seemed so proud of themselves. They had typed them up on their old typewriter, signed them, and even had them witnessed. It was pretty basic. I seem to recall the wills saying that my brother, Terry, and I would split everything equally. Mom and Dad told us that the way they figured it, the business was worth about the same amount as their other assets. Because Terry worked in the shop, they thought he should get the shop and I should get the house and the bank accounts. They made us both co-executors.

Terry and I started asking them questions about the wills: What happens if we don't agree on something? Didn't they want to leave something to Mom's cousin, Jennifer, to whom they had been sending money? What happens if Terry or I die? They gave us a blank stare. At that point, we asked them why they didn't just go to a lawyer. Dad didn't want to pay the money. He thought that he could do just as good a job as any lawyer. After all, he had been the executor of both of his parents' estates. Mom was nervous about going to a lawyer. She had never met a lawyer before. She wasn't even sure she had the proper clothes to wear to a lawyer's office. It took a while, but Terry and I convinced them that they needed to have a professional draft their wills.

The next time we were all together, Dad and Mom said that they had been to see a lawyer and that he was drafting their wills. Dad still didn't seem convinced that the lawyer could do a better job than he could, but that was just Dad. We were happy that they had finally gotten some legal assistance.

Our parents didn't offer to show us the wills the lawyer drafted, and we didn't ask to see them. Once we knew that they had been to a lawyer, we didn't really care what they did from there.

Dad, Mom, and Terry died in an accident together. When I went through their house to look for their wills, I found a file marked "estate plan." In it was an advertisement from a magazine offering "Wills starting at $199." I shook my head and smiled. Clearly if Dad was going to have to use a lawyer, he was not going to pay for one of those "high-rent-district big shots." I called the lawyer and made an appointment to meet with him.

The sinking feeling started as I pulled up to the lawyer's office. The sign out front read: "Bankruptcies—$299, Wills—$199, and Divorces—$399." When I sat down with the lawyer, things just got worse. He told me that Mom's cousin Jennifer got 25 percent of the estate, and that Terry and I split the rest. I had to remind him, again, that Terry had died in the same accident. Since Terry was dead, he told me that Terry's wife would be the beneficiary of Terry's portion. That made no sense to me. Terry and his wife had been living apart for two years. They were not legally separated, but there were enough hard feelings that I was very surprised that my parents would put such a provision in their wills. When I asked the lawyer why my parents left money to Terry's wife, he answered that it was a standard provision in all of his documents—a deceased child's spouse inherits the deceased child's share of the estate. Clearly, he did not discuss this provision for Dad and Mom.

As I read the wills, I realized that things were even worse than the lawyer explained. The wills didn't say that cousin Jennifer got 25 percent and Terry's wife and I split the rest. It said that Mom's cousin Jennifer got 25 percent, Terry's wife got the shop and I got the rest. It was time to be surprised again. Written the way they were, the wills had Jennifer's share deplete my portion of the estate and not Terry's portion. The lawyer said that Dad and Mom wanted to make sure that Terry got the shop, so this was the only way he could ensure that Jennifer got 25 percent of the estate and Terry got the shop. I asked him why he couldn't require that Terry just make up the difference by taking out a loan against the shop. He said he hadn't thought of that, but that it could have solved this problem. I then asked him if my parents understood that this meant I would only be getting about 25 percent of the estate. He said that they didn't specifically discuss it, but that he was sure that they understood. My parents were uneducated, working-class people, and he was sure they understood!

At first I was angry with my parents for going to a lawyer who clearly did not know what he was doing. After a while, I realized that my parents weren't to blame. They thought they were doing the right thing. My mother had never even met a lawyer before. I am sure she thought that if he was a lawyer, he had to know what he was doing. Clearly, she was wrong.

Getting the Right Assistance

You need to choose a lawyer who is competent. You should feel confident that your lawyer will draft your estate plan to reflect your best intentions. Here are five characteristics you should look for in an estate planning attorney:

1. *Good educational background.* Not all attorneys are educated alike. An attorney from a well-established law school is more likely to provide valuable insight as well as sound drafting skills than someone from a weaker law school. Attorneys with LL.M. degrees in taxation or estate planning are more likely to have stronger skills than attorneys who stopped their education after receiving their law degree. An LL.M. is a master of laws, which means that the attorney has taken an extra year of courses in a specialized area.

2. *Experience.* Estate planning is not a black-and-white area of the law. It takes some time and experience to understand a client's needs. Any lawyer can draft a will, but it takes some time to learn how to draft a will that properly reflects a person's intentions. There is no rule of thumb on how long it takes a lawyer to learn these skills, but it is probably safe to say that there needs to be at least a couple of years of full-time work in this area before an attorney can become skilled enough to know the right questions to ask clients. It is also helpful for a lawyer to see an estate plan through to its fruition. How do you know the drafted documents are any good if the lawyer hasn't had any clients who have died?

3. *Specialization in estate planning law.* An attorney who practices medical malpractice law, criminal defense law, and estate planning is not spending enough time in the area of estate planning to excel in the field. You should always ask

how much of an attorney's time is devoted to estate planning. Another way to ask the question is to ask how many wills and trusts the attorney drafts per month. If the answer is less than five, it is probably safe to assume that estate planning is not his or her sole means of support.

4. *Additional credentials beyond the law degree.* Look for an LL.M. degree, a certified specialist designation (many states allow attorneys to hold themselves out as specialists only after he or she has demonstrated extreme competency in his or her field), or membership in ACTEC (American College of Trust and Estates Counsel). ACTEC members must have been practicing law for ten or more years and be recognized for their contributions to estate planning through writing and speaking endeavors.

5. *Trustworthiness.* Does your intuition tell you your estate planning attorney is someone who will be there when your spouse or other family members die? This is someone with whom you will need to share your intimate family secrets, if you are going to develop a plan that is tailored to your family. You want someone who can be trusted and with whom you, your spouse, your children, and your other loved ones feel comfortable.

After you have chosen a lawyer, make sure you read *and understand* the documents he or she prepares for you. There will always be some legal jargon that is hard to get through, but you need to understand whether or not your intentions are reflected in the documents. Your attorney should prepare a summary letter that is in English, not legalese, describing your estate planning documents. If your attorney does not prepare such a letter as a matter of practice, you should ask for one. Without a succinct summary, how will you know whether the documents properly reflect your intentions? It is not *your* estate plan until it says what *you* want it to say.

2

Sweating the Small Stuff

MARIE'S STORY

Pete and I started dating in our 40s. We had both been through pretty tough divorces, and we were both skittish about marriage. We eventually started living together. I suppose we felt that there would be less chance of getting hurt again if we weren't married. Pete and I had lived together for nearly 15 years when he died. We had a good relationship with each other and with each other's children.

Pete was a good man, but he was a procrastinator. I had talked to him until I was blue in the face about drafting new wills that would protect us from each other's children. We had heard so many horror stories from our friends, and I was preparing for the worst. Pete just kept making one excuse after another: "Our kids aren't like so-and-so's kids." "We don't have anything that the kids would want anyway." "Why worry about dying, we are young." Pete had a heart attack getting ready for work one morning. He was 59.

At first everything went fairly smooth. Our house was in joint tenancy, so it immediately became mine. Pete's stock and bank accounts were transferred to his children, as his sole heirs. I thought that took care of everything. I couldn't believe it when his children started asking me about the household furniture. Sure, some of the stuff was Pete's from before we met, but it wasn't worth much—an old bureau, several shelves of books, and our bedroom set. Most of the rest was either given to us or we bought it together.

Pete's children wanted all of Pete's things—including the bed I was sleeping on! They wanted a complete inventory of the household items, right down to the blue-and-white-striped towels that Christa claimed she had given to her father but not to me. When I couldn't account for some of the things Pete had been given by his children over the years, they accused me of stealing. It was more likely that Pete donated them to the local homeless shelter.

I am sure their mother was behind most of their behavior. She never did like the fact that Pete and I were living together. Even with all of her bitterness, I never expected a lawsuit. The children filed a lawsuit claiming that I had stolen items of Pete's that were rightfully theirs. The list was over 150 items long. Because the children had all of Pete's money, I only had my small savings to use to hire a lawyer. In the end, the lawyer advised me that because the children were so adamant about the "stuff," and because I didn't have the resources to fight them, I should settle.

I sold the house, offered them a cash settlement for the things I could not find, and gave them most of the rest of the items on the list. I am renting right now. I hope to find a small condominium soon. In the meantime, I have bought a new bedroom set, but the bed is not as comfortable as Pete's bed.

Personalizing Your Personal Effects

A lot of people think that only people with very large estates need to do estate planning. That kind of thinking is just plain wrong. Although it may be true that people with very large estates need to do more complicated estate planning, *everyone* needs to do some planning. Do you know what happens to your possessions without you specifying how they are to be dispersed in your estate plan? Without giving your heirs some sort of direction, there are going to be conflicting claims. In our discussions with estate planning attorneys, litigation attorneys, and heirs, the most common source of disagreements involves the personal effects of the decedent. It is not the big-ticket items—the house, brokerage accounts, and retirement plans—but the grandfather clock, mother's opal earrings, or the oil painting over the mantle that become the center of rifts among family members.

In Pete's case, he probably wanted Marie to have his personal effects rather than his natural heirs, his children. It is important to remember that when your intended beneficiaries are different from your natural beneficiaries, only a will or trust will ensure that the proper people inherit.

Not every case results in litigation. Sometimes, family members stop speaking to each other for years. Part of the problem is that most people, even when they do put together an estate plan, leave personal effects "equally" to the children. Because it wouldn't be practical for each child to take one-third of the grandfather clock or split its use every four months, *equal* comes to mean equal in value. But value, when it comes to personal effects, rarely has anything to do with money. Dividing personal effects equally among the children could really turn out to be anything but equal. And, who makes the decision as to what is an equitable division?

THOMAS'S STORY

Pauline, Joanne, and I were all pretty close growing up. We lost a brother to leukemia at eight, and I think it made us all appreciate each other more than most siblings. As we grew older, we got married and moved to different parts of the country. We didn't have many opportunities to see each other over the years, although we did keep in touch by phone. Sure, there were family reunions every couple of years, but there was not much time at those events to do more than get reacquainted before we were all flying back to our respective homes. When Dad died last year, we all got to know each other better than we wanted.

Dad left a small handwritten will that left everything equally to the three of us. "Everything" sounds like he actually had something to leave. When Mom got sick a few years ago, Dad and Mom had to dip into their savings to pay for the medical expenses. By the time Mom died, they had gone through all of their savings, and Dad even had to mortgage the house. All that was really left at Dad's death was about $14,500 equity in the house, $750 in the bank, a $10,000 life insurance policy Dad took out when he was in the Navy, and the contents of the house. The cash was used to pay for the funeral and burial and some outstanding bills. After that, the only things left to be divided were the items in the house. That's where the problems began.

It started innocently enough. Joanne mentioned that Mom had told her years ago that because she was the older daughter she could have the china set that came from England with Mom's mother when she emigrated to the United States. Pauline also wanted the china set. Pauline has always been the family historian, tracking our genealogy back seven generations. She told us how she and Mom used to sit down and talk about the stories her mother had told her about life in England at the turn of the century. It had meant so much to her to have a piece of the family history that she had gone to Dad after Mom's death and asked for the china. Dad told Pauline she could have it.

Pauline could not understand why Joanne would want something that would mean so much more to Pauline. She was upset that Joanne was now making such a big deal over it. Joanne, on the other hand, felt like the china was the one thing she had that was special from Mom, that Mom had thought she would like. I tried to stay out of the fray, but both of my sisters looked to me to take sides. A decision had to be made, and as much as I hated doing it, I said that I thought the set should be Joanne's, because Mom had promised it to her.

I haven't heard from Pauline all year—no Christmas card, no call on my birthday. When I called on her birthday, her husband said she was unavailable. I left a message, but she didn't return my call. I saw Joanne about six months ago, when I was in her city for business. When I noticed that she did not replace the china in her cabinet with Mom's china, I mentioned it to her. She said that Mom's china had more dings and nicks than her other china, so she was not going to display it. I could have strangled her!

I will keep trying to mend my relationship with Pauline. I don't know if Joanne will be able to mend it with either of us. Imagine—all of this over an old, beat-up set of china.

There are several ways to go about planning for the distribution of personal effects. Here are a few of the better ones, certainly a few of the more creative solutions we have come across:

- *Make a list of all of the items of value in your home and assign beneficiaries to each of them.* If you spell out who gets what, you will minimize the chance of disagreements among your beneficiaries. However, there are a couple of problems with this solution. First, just because you value only certain items does not mean that other items may not have value to your heirs. Unless you plan to itemize every item in your house, you may inadvertently leave off the list the one item in dispute. Second, this type of a list requires constant updating. If you buy something new or get rid of something on the list, you could be in the same position as not having done the list at all. Lots of squabbles begin over items that show up on a list but no longer exist. If there is already potential for distrust (for example, a second marriage situation), it is easy to imagine accusations of theft. Finally, you may assign the master bedroom bureau to one child and the guest bedroom bureau to another child—exactly opposite of what they would have wanted. Sometimes, the mere act of reducing these items to writing inhibits beneficiaries from asking for an alternative distribution. After all, "if Dad wanted me to have this one, then I have to honor his wishes."

- *Tag items in the house with people's names now.* We know several people who have done this and say it works great. If a child sees his name on something he does not want, or missing from something he does want, he has the opportunity to say something now. Again, there are a couple of possible problems with this solution. First, if you change names around over time, someone whose name was once on the dining room table may wrongly accuse the new recipient of wrongdoing. Second, it may not be practical at

age 30, 40, or 50 to begin labeling all of your assets antici-
pating your death.

• *Set up a system to draw lots.* Drawing lots ensures each of the
  children has an opportunity to get what he or she wants
  without letting emotions play a disproportionate role in
  the decision-making process. Some people suggest having
  the selection process done room by room to avoid the situation where one person selects a pair of cheap earrings
  and another person selects the entire living room set.

• *Design a resolution system in the event of disputes.* Assuming
  you want the beneficiaries to decide among themselves,
  still plan for what should happen in the event of a dispute.
  My husband and I are the proud owners of a very unique
  and very old piano. We purchased the piano at an estate
  sale for one-tenth of its value. At first we figured there had
  to be something wrong with the piano, but it turned out
  there was nothing wrong with it. What was "wrong" was
  that all of the beneficiaries had wanted the piano, and
  none of them would budge on the issue. Rather than pro-
  longing the family feud, the executor decided to sell it
  quickly and simply divide the proceeds. It turned out that
  this piano was rich in national history. If the parents had
  set up a system to resolve disputes, even if as rudimentary
  as drawing the high card, maybe the piano also could have
  become rich in their family history.

Protecting Your Tiniest Treasures

Doing an estate plan is especially important for people with
young children. Until your children turn 18, one of the greatest
responsibilities you have towards them is deciding who will take
care of them if you are no longer here. If you do not take the
steps necessary to appoint a guardian, your children can wind up

in the last place you would ever choose. Most states have a priority system that determines who is entitled to become the guardian of your children. Generally, the surviving parent has priority, even if he or she is not the custodial parent. Remember, under California's priority system, O.J. Simpson became the guardian of his minor children. After the surviving parent, typically the grandparents have priority, followed by the children's aunts and uncles. If you do not want your parents or your spouse's parents to raise your children, you need to do something about it.

Even worse, each level of priority can encompass several people, all of whom may fight to become the guardian of your children. And it's possible they are none of the people you would have selected yourself. Although a legislative priority system has some merit in that it lessens the chances of squabbles by naming who has first rights to become guardian, I cannot imagine leaving a decision like that to legislators. Imagine the following: You are the parent of two young children. You and your spouse spend weekends at soccer games and weeknights working on arithmetic problems. You haven't gone on a vacation alone for the last four years, because you like to spend your time away from the office with your kids. You finally decide that now is the time to take a trip together—just the two of you. Right before you go, you drive down to the state capitol building, locate the representative from your district, and ask him to name the guardian of your children should you and your spouse die on this trip. Can you imagine anything more ridiculous? Probably not. But, that is exactly what you are doing, if you do not name a guardian for your children in your will.

A few years ago, there was a guardianship dispute that made most of the television newsmagazines. The story went something like this: Jack and Jill were married, and Jill was pregnant with their first child. During the pregnancy, Jill discovered she had cancer. Jack and Jill prepared wills and named Jill's brother as guardian for their unborn child. Jill's parents were named as successor guardians. Jill gave birth to a healthy daughter, but the cancer had progressed to an advanced and fatal stage. Several months later, Jill died. Jack, after telling his parents that he only named Jill's family as guardians so as not to upset Jill, ripped up his will. Before his daughter had even reached her first birthday, Jack was killed in a car accident. The question then became, Who would become the guardian of the young girl? Both Jack's parents and Jill's parents petitioned the court for guardianship. The provision in Jill's will naming her brother was no longer effective, because she predeceased Jack. The provision in Jack's will was not effective because he ripped up his will. A huge court battle ensued. In time, Jill's brother even got involved in the case as a potential guardian. The families took the case all the way to the Supreme Court of their state.

In the end, it really didn't matter who actually became guardian. What did matter was that by having no provisions in place, families who otherwise could have been bonding together to raise this child were fighting each other in court. And, ultimately, the daughter may not have wound up with the guardian her parents had wanted for her.

Knowing that you need to select a guardian is one thing; actually making the selection is another. It is hard to imagine anyone else raising your children, but it is even harder imagining the wrong person raising your children. There are a few important things on which to focus when deciding on a guardian for your children:

- The guardian only needs to get your children through the age of majority (age 18, in most states). If you were ruling out people because of age (for example, the grandparents), you may want to reconsider.

- If you are thinking of a couple (for example, your sister and brother-in-law), is it really both people you intend to name? What if your sister predeceases you? Do you really want your brother-in-law as guardian? Or, do you only want your children raised by a married couple and not by either person individually?

- Who is your choice as secondary guardian? It may have been difficult to choose an initial guardian, but you should always have a second choice just in case.

- If your children are in school, does your guardian live in the same area, so that your children do not have to change schools? If not, would your guardian be willing *and* able to move so as not to further disrupt your children's lives?

- Does your guardian share your same thoughts about church, education, or responsibility? Sometimes people only focus on family members as guardians, even though there may be others who are more closely aligned with their beliefs on child rearing. Your guardian will, after all, be the one raising your children.

- Does your guardian have a good relationship with your family and with your spouse's family? If not, will the guardian encourage relationships and visits with those family members?

- Are there additional messages you want to leave for your guardians or for the people you didn't name as guardian? For example, maybe you want to give the reasons why you made your selection. Or maybe you want to encourage your guardian to move into your home. You may want to make sure that the guardian understands that visits with "crazy" Uncle Joe should be supervised.

Also, keep in mind the consequences of making guardianship contingent on certain specified events. Suppose that you name your sister as guardian of your four-year-old and six-year-old but only on the condition that she never move the children from their home. What if ten years later, with the wholehearted approval of the children, your sister takes a new job requiring her to move to another city? Are you really going to have the children removed from her care at that point? If you have particular desires, state them but try not to make them a condition of guardianship. Otherwise, your children will have lost their parents and may also be taken away from the person you entrusted them to at your death. Just think through the consequences.

If you don't do an estate plan, because your estate is "too small," then you have given up the opportunity to override the priority in the law as to who will be the guardian of your children. Instead, you will have placed that decision in the hands of legislators. By not picking the guardian yourself, you may have started a family war that could only add to the children's pain of losing their parents.

Man's Best Friend—Dead or Alive

Sometimes, the most cherished item you own is also a member of your family. No, we don't mean to imply that you own your spouse, your children, your parents, or some other member of your blood relations. We're talking about your pets. If you have pets, you know what we mean. Even if you think your estate is too small to worry about any planning, have you given any thought to who will take care of your dog, cat, or other pet when you die? Do you want to make sure some of your money goes to the care of your pet?

NORMA'S STORY

My friend Norma had always been a dog lover. Actually, dog lover is not a strong enough term to describe Norma. She didn't just love dogs, she was someone who would take in strays, find homes for them, and then check up on them until she was sure they were fine. Since I'd known Norma, she had always lived with at least three dogs. She used to say, "Human roommates need not apply." Norma was fanatical about making sure her dogs were cared for in the event something happened to her. She even had her estate plan drafted to provide for her dogs in case she died. She told me once that this became a crusade for her after she heard about a friend who had died leaving a dog. Apparently, none of her friend's family members wanted the dog. They couldn't find a home for it, and had it put to sleep. Norma said that she never wanted that to happen to her "babies."

Norma had her lawyer draft a provision in her trust that any family member who took in her dogs would receive all of Norma's assets. The assets would remain in a trust while the dogs were alive. The trustee of the trust, her veterinarian, would be responsible for checking on the dogs once a month. The visits were to be unannounced. If the dogs were healthy and well treated, the trustee would make a cash distribution from the trust to the family member. If they were being mistreated in any way, the trustee would remove the dogs from the family member's care and transfer the funds to a trust for any other family member willing to care for the dogs. If no one in Norma's family wanted the dogs, the trustee would find a good home for them and then distribute the remaining funds to the humane society. When the last of the dogs had died (of natural causes), the remaining money would be paid to the family member who cared for them. All costs of maintaining the dogs (for example, grooming, feeding, and veterinarian bills) would be paid from the trust. Norma figured that the incentive of getting the money would keep the dogs well cared for.

Norma was not wealthy by any means. I think when she died she left about $70,000. Her brother David, who was never much of an animal lover, agreed to take the dogs. He actually did a great job looking after the dogs, and in time I think he actually came to really care for them. I am sure this was Norma's intention all along.

You cannot name your pet as a direct beneficiary of your estate. However, this does not mean that you cannot come up with any number of creative provisions to care for your pets. Certainly, Norma's decision to make the inheritance contingent on someone properly caring for her dogs is one such provision. But, you could just as easily leave your $1,000 estate or $1,000,000 estate to the person who is willing to care for your pets. Or, you could leave the money in a trust that provides that any expenses are reimbursed to the person who has taken your pets. Some more unique conditions, such as the pet has to be allowed to eat from the family table or sleep in a person's bed before distributions will be permitted, may be difficult to monitor.

Your Estate Is Never Too Small

When there is not much in the way of assets, we often hear people ask why they need to complicate things by doing an estate plan. Even in the smallest estates, an estate plan clarifies and sometimes even protects the intentions of the deceased.

BETTY'S STORY

After years of living from paycheck to paycheck as a single mother, Betty was finally able to put some money into a savings account at the bank. She was also able to purchase her first new car. Her children, Alex and Brett, were working and starting their own lives. Everything finally started to fall into place for Betty. Betty and I attended church together. One night, we had a person come and speak about planning our estates. I remember that after the meeting Betty thought nothing in the speech really applied to her. She didn't have much of an estate, so why would she complicate her life by putting together some "fancy-shmancy" plan. Besides, it was a waste of her hard-earned money and something she could take care of herself. She told me that she put Alex on both her savings account and her car and that when she died, he would just split the money with Brett. She didn't put Brett's name on anything, because he had been in trouble a few times in the past. Alex was a good kid, so it seemed to make a lot of sense.

Alex was 25 when Betty died. Brett was 23. Alex told me at the funeral that he needed to get his mother's things together, so he could figure out how much to give to Brett. About two months later, I heard from another friend at church that Alex had an accident while riding his bicycle. The rider of the other bike had broken his back and sued Alex for riding recklessly. Apparently, all of Betty's money was frozen until the lawsuit was settled. It looked like the injured rider would receive everything, even Brett's share of the money. Even though Alex intended to give Brett his half of the money, the lawsuit came along before he had a chance. Because Brett wasn't named on the accounts, he had no rights to the money. Neither did the two young children he was struggling to support. Not only did Alex lose but so did Brett (and Betty's grandchildren).

I think it is interesting that people with small estates are much less likely to do estate planning than people with large estates. Of course, the larger estates need to plan for tax and probate issues that smaller estates may never need to consider. But, quite often, the beneficiaries of smaller estates are in much greater need of the funds. Brett really could have used his half of Betty's estate. A proper plan could have ensured that Brett got the money he so badly needed.

It's Just a Small Gift

Sometimes, it is not the estate that is small but the amount you want to pass. It is not uncommon for grandparents to want to give their grandchildren something. Often, they want those gifts to be made now, while the grandparents are still around to help guide the grandchildren. What an opportunity to be able to pass some of your wealth and wisdom today, while you are still alive! Last year, my granddaughter Morgan asked me to guess what she wanted for her sixth birthday. After several unsuccessful answers, an exasperated Morgan informed me: "I want a Barbie doll and stocks, Nana!" Let's face it, the younger generations are more sophisticated than ever before. They are ready and willing to absorb the information we are waiting to share. The problem becomes how to impart our wisdom without putting too much money into a youngster's hands today.

MARTIN'S STORY

We were so grateful when Dad set up custodial accounts for our sons and daughter when they were born. He put in a few thousand dollars each year. He really took a lot of pressure off us toward funding our children's college educations. Our older son was able to pay for his first two years of college with the funds from his custodial account. Our second son paid for his entire art school education with his money.

When each of the kids turned eight, Dad took them to the brokerage firm where he set up the custodial accounts. He showed them their statements and started "talking stocks" with them. Each year, he would schedule a meeting with each child and discuss the strategy for the account. He wanted them to feel like they were really participating in the investment decisions. The kids loved it. Dad loved it too. He said it gave him a chance to spend some time with the kids, teaching them about the value of money.

Our youngest child will be 18 next month, and that is the problem. When Jessica started her senior year of high school this year, everything seemed fine. She was applying to colleges and already talking about graduate school. Looking back, I think the problems started when she started dating Brad. She became withdrawn and uncommunicative. Her grades started to drop, but we thought she just had a case of "senioritis."

About a month ago, she came home in the back of a police car. She had been caught shoplifting at the local mall, and the police suspected that she was under the influence of drugs. When we confronted Jessica, she went crazy. She started yelling and screaming and even threatened to kill us. When she was picked up again a week later with Brad, she was taken to jail. That is where she is right now. We are at a loss over what to do. When she went to jail, we went through her room and found enough evidence to convince us that she was heavily into drugs.

After calling a lawyer regarding Jessica's legal problems, we asked Dad to call his broker to find out how to extend the age on her custodial account. Clearly, we cannot let her get the money out of that account next month. We were shocked to find out there was nothing Dad or we could do. Because the account is set up as a custodial account, the broker informed us that the law required full distribution at age 18.

I am still very grateful to my father for setting up these accounts. How was he to know what was going to happen? But I am also very frustrated, because this money that was supposed to be used to help Jessica may instead be used to hurt her. I may have been naïve in the past, but I know what the money is going to be used for now—more drugs. And there is nothing we can do to stop it.

When dealing with smaller amounts of money, it sometimes seems silly to go to the trouble of paying a lawyer to set up a trust for beneficiaries. Custodial accounts are relatively simple and inexpensive ways of putting money aside for your children and grandchildren when they are too young to have immediate access to the money. Trusts are going to take a bit more time to develop and will also be more expensive. However, trusts will allow you to build as much flexibility into them as you decide. If Martin's father had set up trusts for Jessica and her brothers, he still could have taught them about stocks and had the money growing for their educations. In addition, he could have had provisions allowing Martin to extend the age his children received the money or restricting the use of the money for education only.

Sometimes, the smallest lessons are the most important lessons. Whether you are dealing with personal effects, young children, pets, or just a small estate, it definitely pays to "sweat the small stuff."

CHAPTER

3

It's Hard to Prepare
For the Unexpected

KRISTY'S LETTER

Dear Mom,

It has been 28 years now. It feels like yesterday. I was a know-it-all 16-year-old arguing with you about whether college was appropriate for all people. I remember you telling me that if I didn't get a college degree, I could plan to pump gas for the rest of my life. Mom, you are not going to believe this, but everyone pumps his or her own gas now. Anyway, I guess I wasn't all that surprised when I read your will. Staring me in the face was language saying that if I did not get my college degree within six years of high school graduation, 25 percent of your estate was going to charity; if I did not get my college degree within eight years of high school graduation, 50 percent of your estate was going to charity; and if I did not get my college degree by the age of 30, your entire estate was going to charity. It was as if you were trying to get in the last word in our argument. Of course, at the time you died I was already starting my junior year of college and was on track to graduate within four years of my high school graduation. You had made your point, without the incentives. I already understood the value of a college education.

As you know, Mom, I never wound up receiving any of your estate. While I know what you were trying to accomplish with the provisions in your will, something unexpected happened during my junior year. It was just after semester break, and I was heading back to my apartment after my first day of classes. I was the passenger in a car that was broadsided when some guy ran a red light. I spent two months in intensive care. Among other things, I fractured two vertebrae, my right arm, my right leg, and four ribs, and I punctured a lung. With time and a great deal of physical therapy, I was able to conquer almost all of my physical disabilities. My studies, of course, suffered. It took me five years to return to college and another three years to actually graduate. By that time, I had just turned 30. It would have been nice to receive an inheritance at that time. I managed to survive. I know you were trying to do the best for me. It's okay, though, I know it is hard to plan for the unexpected.

Love,

Kristy

Life Is Not Static—Why Is Your Plan?

When Carol went to her estate planning attorney, Kristy was 15—before the fight about college. Carol was college educated and felt that it was extremely important for Kristy to be educated as well. Carol also thought that if Kristy "took a break" from school, she might never finish. After talking to her estate planning attorney about these concerns, Carol's attorney drafted the provisions requiring Kristy to graduate within a certain time period in order to receive her inheritance. In theory, the clause accomplishes exactly what Carol hoped to accomplish. Kristy would be penalized if she took a break from school.

Creating incentives or penalties to encourage or discourage certain behavior in our children is something we do from the time our children are young. They receive allowances for cleaning their rooms and time-outs when they don't behave. However, we have the flexibility to make changes in our policies as circumstances dictate. If our estate plans are inflexible, then we are faced with situations like the one Kristy faced. Had Carol been alive, would she really have stuck to the age-30 limitation for graduation? Probably not.

How could Carol have done things differently and still maintained the penalties if Kristy took a break from school? Carol could have given her trustee the ability to change the requirements, if he or she thought it would be appropriate. Sometimes, however, this type of unfettered discretion is too broad to give to another person. What if the trustee thinks that a couple of years abroad is a legitimate reason for changing the requirements, but you don't? Alternatively, Carol could have loosened the restriction directly in the document. For example, she could have kept the same language and simply added the phrase, "unless my child is unable due to medical reasons to obtain such bachelor's degree."

How can you make sure that you don't make the same mistake as Carol? Play the "what if" game with each decision you make. What if she doesn't graduate from college because she is ill? What if she doesn't graduate from college but becomes a master chef? What if she is working her way through school and, therefore, is putting her graduation on a longer time schedule? What if the college or university is not accredited? By working through the "what ifs," you will be much more prepared for the unexpected.

And, don't forget that there is more than just money involved when planning your estate—there are lives involved.

SUSAN'S STORY

My brother-in-law Frank always thought everything through. At least it seemed that way to the rest of us. Frank married my sister Vivien 12 years ago. They had two beautiful daughters, Darla, who is ten, and Fiona, who is eight. Frank had one adult child from his previous marriage, Wayne. Wayne was a nice young man who quickly welcomed my sister into his life when she and Frank got married. Shortly after Frank married my sister, he went to his lawyer and had his living trust updated. After each of his daughters was born, he went back to the lawyer to review and update his trust.

Frank provided that his son Wayne would receive a one-third share of the estate immediately on Frank's death. Wayne's share was to stay in trust until he turned 30. Vivien was to receive the balance of Frank's estate. The money was to be kept in a trust for her to live off during her life. At her death, the balance would pass to their two daughters. Until the girls turned 21, the trust provided for their education. From 21 through 30, the trust also provided for all income of the trust to be distributed to the girls, as well as any principal needed for their health, education, and living expenses. At 30, the girls were to receive the balance of their inheritances. It seemed at the time to be a great plan. The girls' education was paid for, the trust would provide for their needs but wouldn't let the girls squander any money during their reckless 20s, and everything would be distributed to them when they reached a responsible age.

Frank spent so much time focusing on what the children were going to get as adults, he forgot to focus on their needs as children. Of course, Frank, like all of us, probably thought he was going to live to see his children reach those ages and beyond. Even if Frank didn't live that long, he knew Vivien would look out for the girls. Then, one foggy night, on the way home from a charity benefit, a drunk driver crossed the center divider and struck Frank and Vivien's car. They died instantly. The estate totaled $12,000,000, after all of the estate taxes were paid. Four million dollars went into Wayne's trust. Darla and Fiona's trusts also received $4,000,000 each.

The girls are living with me. I have my own small house and support them on my preschool teacher's salary. They are not entitled to distributions from their trusts for their health or living expenses. Wayne has indicated a willingness to help his young half-sisters, but the trustee of his trust will not make distributions to Wayne, unless Wayne can prove that he himself is in need of funds. Because Wayne is working, he cannot prove that he is in need of funds.

I have already been advised that to question the provisions of the trust will be treated as if the girls are contesting the trusts and will result in their losing all of their trust funds—forever. For now, I am taking care of the girls as best I can. I just hope that neither of them becomes seriously ill, because I cannot even afford health insurance for them.

Be Prepared—For Anything

Frank's failure to plan for the possibility of both he and his wife dying while their daughters were still young, put his daughters into a situation he could not have intended. While the girls are under 21, their trusts only pay for their education. If one daughter is sick, the trust will not pay for her care. If a daughter needs living expenses, the trust will not pay for a roof over her head or for her food. Once each daughter is 21, all of these items can be paid for from the trust. Do you think Frank really meant to deprive his daughters at ages eight and ten but have the trust give them everything they need at age 24? Probably not.

The first time you packed for camp, your mother probably asked you at least five times if you packed enough underwear. What about your rain gear? Your swimsuit? She wanted to make sure you were prepared for any possibility. It might rain or be warm enough to swim, so you took the extra step of being prepared for anything.

You also need to be prepared for anything when you design your estate plan. We cannot stress enough that you don't know when your time here on earth will come to an end. As a result, you need to be prepared for the possibility that you might not be here tomorrow. You need to think about the following:

- If your beneficiaries are young, how do you want to provide for their support? If your beneficiaries are your nieces and nephews, will you just assume that their parents will take care of their basic needs? What if their parents lose their jobs? You cannot just rely on the assumption that the current state of affairs is going to continue.

- If your beneficiaries are relatives who need the money, would they still be your beneficiaries if they stop needing the money at a later date? Some people will choose only certain brothers and sisters as their beneficiaries, because they have a greater need than other siblings. But what if one of your chosen siblings hits the lottery right before your death? Or, one of the siblings not chosen can no longer work for health reasons? You could specify a net worth standard for your beneficiaries to be able to inherit.

Alternatively, you could leave a sum of money that any "needy" heir could access.

- Have you thought about how your beneficiaries' lives will change over time? Is your estate plan flexible enough to change with them? Children will grow up, go to school, get jobs, and have families of their own. The same provisions that were appropriate at 15 are not likely to be appropriate at 50.

- Do you know enough about your beneficiaries' lives to be sure about the provisions/conditions/restrictions you place in your estate plan? For example, are you leaving money to someone who is considering divorce? Will your inheritance become part of the divorce proceedings?

MACK'S STORY

My parents had a great marriage. They were married 57 years when Mom discovered she had cancer. Dad took care of her until her death 18 months later. Within a year, Dad also died. I think he just didn't know how to live without Mom or didn't want to. I thought I had the same great fortune as my parents with an incredible marriage to Betsey. We had been married 22 years when Dad died.

When Mom got sick, the three of us went to a lawyer to get my parents' affairs in order. We learned all about wills, trusts, powers of attorney, and all sorts of other things. Mom and Dad insisted that as their only child I be involved in every aspect of the planning process. In the end, they decided to leave one-half of their estate to me and the other half to Betsey. They wanted to make sure that Betsey knew how much they loved her. They wanted her to know that they thought of her as a daughter. I really appreciated the gesture. Besides, Betsey and I were one. What was mine was hers, and what was hers was mine. My parents actually had a much harder time deciding what to do about our three sons. They wanted to make sure the boys benefited from some of the wealth they had amassed over the years—nearly $1,000,000. In the end, they decided that Betsey and I would take care of the boys.

I guess I should at least be grateful that my parents died without knowing what type of deception Betsey perpetrated on us. Shortly after we finished paying the estate taxes following Dad's death, I came home to find Betsey gone. I don't mean that she was late returning from shopping or a PTA meeting. She had packed her bags, liquidated the stocks from my parents, took almost $500,000, and moved out. She had been having an affair for about three years with someone she had met at the gym. She left the boys and me and moved in with her new love.

I tried to reason with her, but she said she was just tired of being with the same man she had been with since college. She said she needed to be her own person, separate and apart from her husband and children. No matter what I tried, she refused to reconsider and come back to us.

I have seen Betsey a few times around town since the divorce. She still doesn't come by to see the boys. I've heard that she and her boyfriend went through all of the money my parents left her within a year. Not a penny went to our children.

I was grateful that my parents decided to treat Betsey as part of the family. In retrospect, they should have forgotten about Betsey's feelings and left that portion of the money straight to the boys. It is said that hindsight is 20-20. It is too bad that foresight isn't as clear.

Don't Wait—You May Not Get Another Chance

We both still tear up thinking about all of the people who lost their lives in the World Trade Center and Pentagon bombings. All of those people got up that morning thinking their day was going to be just like the ones before it; none of them expected it would be their last day. So many were young. They were traders and firefighters, servicemen and businesswomen. Some left behind young children. Others hadn't even gotten married or had a chance to start a family. Many had no estate plans in place.

Many of these people died outside of what we normally think of as the natural order. They are survived by parents and in some cases grandparents. We often believe we will outlive our parents and other older relatives, but we can't expect that this will always be the case. We need to consider our unexpected, and untimely, deaths when determining our beneficiaries.

When my husband and I originally planned our estate, we provided only for our two young daughters. We wanted to make sure they were fully taken care of at our deaths. After giving it some thought, we realized that we forgot about my mother. It wasn't intentional; we just didn't think that we might die before her. We thought of all sorts of provisions for the girls if we died while they were still young. Clearly, if we died while our daughters were young, my mother would likely have survived us. We always said that someday my mother would probably move in with us. We expected that we would need to take care of her financially as she got older. If she needed help while we were still living, she would still need help if we were gone. In fact, figuring in our life insurance, we would probably be in an even better position to take care of both the girls and my mother after we died.

You need to look beyond the obvious and the expected when considering who to name as your beneficiaries:

- Do you have parents or grandparents who may need your financial support after your death? Don't leave it all to your siblings assuming that they are more likely to outlive you and will take care of older family members in your stead. They too could die, leaving the money to someone (like a girlfriend or an even younger generation) who does not have the same feelings for your older relatives. Or, they could lose it in a bankruptcy or other financial mishap. Also, they may just not have the same feelings of responsibility toward the older generation as you.

- Is your spouse ill? Leaving assets to your children or other relatives and bypassing your spouse can result in disastrous consequences. The last thing you want to do is leave your sons-in-law and daughters-in-law in charge of determining the type of medical care your spouse can afford. If your children are very young, the matter will be taken out of their hands and put into the hands of someone who faces the risk of a lawsuit if he or she provides for anyone other than your children. For those of you who have cared for a terminally ill loved one, you know that it takes a lot of time, energy, love, *and* money. Why would you take that money away from your spouse at the time when he or she needed it most—at your unexpected death?

- Do you have others who are not your natural heirs (a godchild, a niece or nephew, or a foster child) that you help to support? What would happen to those individuals, if you were no longer here to provide support for them?

ANTHONY'S AND MARCO'S LETTERS

Dear Marco,

Papa Vincent has run out of money, and we need to figure out how to care for him. Stella and I have talked about it, and we agreed that we could move him into our house. We need some money, though. We still have some of the money that Mom and Dad left to me, but not much. We haven't been able to track down Uncle Paulo, but you know he has never been one to count on in a situation like this anyway. I know Mom and Dad thought that we would have enough to take care of Papa Vincent if they died before him, but who thought he would last this long? Could you send us some of the money that Mom and Dad left you? Stella and I think that between what you and I have left, we should be able to manage for a couple of years.

Thanks,

Anthony

Dear Anthony,

I got your letter but am not going to be able to help with Papa Vincent's care. I can't believe you still have money left from Mom and Dad. I ran out of their money in the first year. I'm really not sure why we should be responsible for Papa Vincent. We hardly ever saw him when we were growing up. Besides, if Uncle Paulo isn't making himself available to take care of Papa Vincent, why should we?

By the way, are we still on for that Fourth of July party? I can't wait to see the work you did on the house.

See ya later,

Marco

Dear Marco,

After receiving your letter, Stella and I decided that we could not take this responsibility on by ourselves. We finally tracked down Uncle Paulo, but he is not interested

in helping out either. Since Papa Vincent is virtually pen-
niless, we have decided to put him in a state-run facility.
It is not one of the better places I have seen, but the state
will cover all of his care. We won't have to pay for anything.

Ciao,

Anthony

P.S. Come by before the party to see the new deck we just
put on the back of the house. It is great!

Marco and Anthony's parents may have had their reasons for
not leaving their money to Papa Vincent. Maybe they thought
that at his age he would not know how to handle the money.
Maybe they thought he had enough to take care of himself. Probably, they thought that they would outlive him, and that even if
they did not, their sons would take care of him. You cannot rely
on others to do what you would do. Marco and Anthony's parents
could have provided for Papa Vincent in several different ways to
ensure that he was properly taken care of until his death:

- They could have left Papa Vincent a percentage of their
  estates at their death, with a contingency provision that if
  Papa Vincent predeceased them the money would go to
  Marco and Anthony. However, one problem with this solution is that if Papa Vincent outlived them but didn't spend
  the money before his death, he could leave it to anyone he
  wanted—including the cute young nurse caring for him.

- They could have left some money in a trust for Papa Vincent with a contingency provision that if Papa Vincent predeceased them the money would go to Marco and Anthony.
  This would still allow Papa Vincent to have money for his
  care but would ensure that any money left at Papa Vincent's
  death would go straight to Marco and Anthony (not the

pretty nurse). One problem with this solution is that once the money in Papa Vincent's trust is spent (even if only for his medical and living expenses), it is gone, and Papa Vincent will again be in the position of having no money.

- They could have left their entire inheritance in trust for Papa Vincent, Marco, and Anthony. While Papa Vincent was still living, the trust could provide for his care. At his death, the trust could be divided between Marco and Anthony and distributed to them. This way, there would be no fear that Marco and Anthony would spend the money needed to care for Papa Vincent. The problem with this solution is that all of the money in the trust could be used for Papa Vincent's care, leaving nothing for Marco and Anthony at his death.

Even though the above solutions each have particular problems, the results are significantly better than what actually happened in real life. We can't predict when we will die or who will survive us. We need to base our estate plans on assumptions and contingencies that may or may not occur. We have to prepare for the unexpected. But, at least if we have thought through the possibilities, we will be much closer to fulfilling our best intentions.

4

Hard Work Never Killed Anybody

KELLY'S STORY

I guess I've always been a little jealous of Kelly. When we were growing up, I had to work a part-time job in high school to earn enough money for a car. It was ten years old, full of rust holes, and a huge gas guzzler. We used to call it the "blue boat." Kelly's grandparents had set up a trust fund for her. When she turned 16, she got a beautiful silver Corvette—definitely not a "boat."

When we went to college, I was up to my ears in student loans. Even with the student loans, I still had to sell my bed one semester to be able to afford to eat. Kelly's trust fund paid for her school. She lived in a fancy apartment off-campus and always had plenty of extra spending money. I couldn't figure out why, with all of those extras, it still took her two years longer than me to graduate.

It took me ten years to pay off those student loans. Boy, did it feel great! I had really become self-sufficient. Kelly kind of jumped from project to project during those ten years. Of course, she never had to work. Her trust fund paid for her new house, all of her bills, even two new cars after she crashed each of her other ones. In spite of everything she has, Kelly never seems satisfied with her life or herself. Maybe I am not so jealous of Kelly after all.

Speak for Yourself and Your Family

Rarely does someone walk into a lawyer's office and say: "When I die, I want my children to become trust fund babies." So, why is it that we often walk out of our lawyers' offices with estate plans that will enable our children to become exactly that— trust fund babies? Why is there a difference between what we want and what we get? The primary reason is because lawyers tend to point their clients in the direction that most closely mirrors the forms they already have drafted on their computers. Who are we to ask for something different? Most of us do not practice law or understand the complexities of estate planning.

In my own estate planning practice, I have discovered over the years that if I present a particular option favorably, most clients will elect that option, even when it does not reflect their intentions. For example, if a person has young children, I may suggest having distributions to the children in stages, such as one-third at age 25, one-third at 30, and one-third at 35. After all, if the children blow the money at 25 and 30, there is still money left at 35. Sounds pretty good, doesn't it? However, this scheme doesn't consider any of the family's personal needs or problems. Maybe the youngest child has a drug problem that would only be worsened with distributions starting at age 25. Or, maybe the oldest child is married to an abusive spouse who will just take control of the money and then file for divorce when the last distribution is made at age 35. Every family is unique, and every estate plan should also be unique.

In addition, most people do not spend a lost of time working out the intricacies of what they want to see happen after their death. Actually, most people have a hard enough time just going in and getting their estate plans done in the first place. If you are going to create an estate plan, do it right. Do not rely on your lawyer to draft something that reflects your visions and ideals. Do not let him or her circumvent your intentions. Tell your lawyer what to draft. The estate planning laws are not so complicated that you cannot get a document that is a reflection of you and your family. The real question is, Where do you start?

1. Write down the things that are most important to you. Is it education? Is it self-reliance? Is it social responsibility?

2. Once you decide what is important to you, how would you foster those values in your beneficiaries when you are still living? If you value education, how about using incentives to encourage your children to get a college degree? If you value self-reliance, would you give your children everything they want, whenever they want it? Or, would you make them work for some things?

3. Think about how your beneficiaries might interpret your words to get around the rules. There are numerous cases of beneficiaries (or their lawyers) coming up with interesting interpretations of the meanings of words used in estate planning documents. If education means tuition only at an accredited four-year college or university, say that. Once you are gone, the words you use in your estate plan are all that can speak for you.

College or Bust

For many people, education is an important value. Parents want to see their children get an education, and grandparents want to ensure that their grandchildren get an education. With more than eight years of post-high-school education each, we both have a strong desire to encourage young people to get a good education. In fact, both of us have included provisions for education of our children and grandchildren. But, because Colleen's focus is more on her young children and Victoria's focus is more on her young grandchildren, the provisions we have included in our estate plans for education are significantly different.

RAY'S STORY

Ray and I served together in the Army more than 40 years ago. We became friends and stayed friends until Ray died several years ago. Just before Ray's wife got cancer and died a couple of years earlier, she and Ray created a living trust. When Ray asked if I would be the successor trustee of the trust, I told him that I was not the person for the job. I didn't think I had the financial background to act as trustee. Ray said I could hire advisors, but that he would only feel comfortable if I was overseeing the investments and administering the distributions. Ray explained that the trust would make things easier on the heirs.

I agreed to act as successor trustee. When Ray died, I hired an investment consultant, an attorney, and an accountant to help me with my duties as trustee. I was shocked and more than a little disappointed to find that the financial portion was the easiest part of acting as trustee. It was less than a month after Ray died that I started getting calls from the beneficiaries. Actually, it was worse than that. Ray had left almost all of his money (nearly $100,000) in trust for some very young grandnieces and grandnephews. The calls were from their parents.

In the beginning, the questions were fairly innocuous: "How will we know what investments you are investing in? What procedures will you require us to follow to get a distribution for our children?" All were reasonable questions as far as I was concerned. The trust was pretty clear about distributing money. Until the grandnieces and grand-nephews either graduated from college or turned 25, whichever came first, payments could only be made for a beneficiary's education. Ray was always a stickler about getting a college education. I think he always felt he had been held back at work—and in life—because he had never gone to college. We used to have philosophical discussions after Sunday dinners together about the necessity of a college degree. I explained to the beneficiaries' parents that I was investing the money on a roughly 15-year growth horizon, because the beneficiaries were between two years old and seven years old. This would give me a decent amount of money to pay for each beneficiary's college education.

The parents asked for copies of the trust, which I gladly sent them. They then began to question my investment strategy. They wanted to know why I thought that I should invest with such a "long-term" strategy in mind. I was confused by the question, because I thought it was clear that the idea was to grow the money for their children's college educations. It didn't take long before it all became clear to me. They asked for distributions to pay for their children's private preschools and elementary schools. They cited to me the boilerplate definition of "education" in the trust. Although I knew Ray wanted the money to be used for college education, nothing in the trust said that was his intention. When I talked to the lawyers, they said I was in a lose-lose situation. The trust was not specific regarding the type of education Ray intended, so if I refused to give them the money now, they could go to court and force the distribution. On the other hand, if I made the requested distributions, the beneficiaries could sue me at a later date if there was not enough money when it came time to go to college.

I had not agreed to act as trustee so I could put myself in the position of being sued. I read and reread the trust. For a guy who couldn't say enough about a college education after those Sunday night dinners, Ray said almost nothing about it in his trust. According to the lawyers, the trust only would have had to say that the primary intent was for the money to be used for *college* education.

It would have cost a lot to fight the beneficiaries' parents. I gave them the money. The trust did say, after all, to pay for their educations. I was Ray's friend for 40 years. I know in my heart he couldn't possibly have meant to pay for private kindergarten.

What do *you* mean when you say you want to pay for education? How likely is it that your definition is the same as your lawyer's definition?

- Does education mean education at any level? Do private elementary school and high school count? Does it include a master's, doctorate, or some other postgraduate degree? Does it apply to vocational as well as academic institutions?

- Do payments for education include room and board (on campus or off campus)? Books (new or used)? A computer (what kind)? Transportation expenses (around campus or only to and from home at break)?

- Are there any additional conditions or restrictions? Can the funds be used to pay for multiple degrees? At the same level (e.g., three bachelor's degrees)? Does a particular grade point average need to be maintained? What about a certain number of credit hours per semester?

JAMIE'S STORY

My friend Jamie had the best deal in town. When his grandfather died, he left a trust that was supposed to pay for his education. Jamie said it was his meal ticket. He said that because the trust didn't explain what qualified as education, he was demanding that anything related to his education applied. He was having the trust pay for his rent, food, car payments, and necessary "spending money." Once he even submitted a bill for a garage door opener, telling the trustee that he had a bad back and if he hurt his back opening the door by hand he would not be able to attend school. What a life!

I don't remember exactly when the trustee finally figured out that Jamie had been registering for classes each semester but not attending any of them. He would take the refund money for the tuition and use it for parties. It was at least a few years into the deal before they caught on. I hope my grandfather leaves me some money for my education, too.

Remember, once you have decided what is important to you, you need to determine how to foster those values in your beneficiaries. Obviously, Jamie did not have the same values about education as his grandfather. If his grandfather had provided for tuition only, Jamie wouldn't have been able to manipulate the trust to pay for so many extras. This wouldn't have helped with the registration scam, however. If his grandfather had given the trustee direction not to make distributions without a full review of Jamie's course loads and grades, this problem, too, could have been avoided.

LINDA'S STORY

My cousin Doris hired a lawyer to prepare her will after both of her sons were already grown. When she died, they were both in their early 30s. They were both fairly well established by then. Glenn, her older son, was married and had three children. He owned his own landscaping company. Greg, the younger one, was still single and was working as a freelance reporter. He had already had a couple of articles printed in some small publications.

Doris's will created trusts for each of the boys that would distribute her assets to them when they turned 40. She said it was always good to make a person pay his own way. Before age 40, the money in the boys' trusts could be used to pay for their health, support, and education, but only after considering their other resources.

Immediately after Doris's death, Greg went back to school. He said that at 32 he didn't feel he was "going anywhere" in his job, so he thought it was time to try something else. For the past seven years, he has been attending college, getting good grades, and changing his major on a regular basis. Since the trust will pay for education, he seems to be content to continue to be educated until he turns 40. The trust is funding everything, and it doesn't look like he is ever going to get his degree.

Glenn, who was 34, shut down his company and decided to go to music school. He said landscaping didn't make him complete. He wanted to finally "live his dream of becoming a serious musician." The school was five days per week for two years. He lasted six months in the program before he quit. The prepaid tuition for the two years was forfeited.

Personally, I think it is a shame that the boys took something that Doris valued, like a good education, and turned it into a joke.

The interesting thing about Linda's story is that Doris really did not value her sons getting an education. When Doris went to the lawyer, she explained that she wanted the money tied up until the boys turned 40. She explained that she always thought that the only way her sons were going to become men was to have them make their own way in the world. She thought that by the time they turned 40, they would have made something of themselves. Why didn't Doris's will reflect her intentions? Although her lawyer may have been listening to Doris, he probably didn't *hear* her. His typical wills and trusts always provided for the health, education, and support of a beneficiary prior to final distribution. He rationalized that clients would not want a beneficiary to be unable to receive medical treatments or have to live on the streets when there was money in the trust that could be used to provide for them. Maybe he was right. The only reason education was part of the trust was because the IRS generally approves of trusts that use the terms *health, education, support,* and *maintenance.* In other words, it was just a boilerplate provision that he put in all of his documents.

Linda was wrong when she said that the boys turned something Doris valued, education, into a joke. Doris did *not* value education, at least not where it concerned her sons. Our point is that you need to make sure your lawyers know what you believe, what you value, and what you intend your estate plans to accomplish. Then, you need to read what they write and make sure you understand what it says. You will not be there to correct misinterpretations. You do not want people to think you value, say, a college education, when you actually believe that college degrees are overrated. Your estate plan is your voice after your death. You need to make sure it speaks the words you intend.

Hard Work Develops Character

My husband and I agree that we would never have been as successful as we are if everything had just been handed to us along the way. Our parents made us get jobs in high school, and

we worked our way through college and law school. It was not
easy, and there were times when it would have been great to have
been handed enough cash and not have to work. But, working
our way through school made us appreciate our educations and
gave us the strength to work hard after we graduated. Now we
are faced with our toughest challenge. How do we teach our
daughters to be self-reliant, when a part of us wants to just give
them what we have worked for so hard?

It is our job to make sure that our daughters become self-reliant, productive members of society. We just are not convinced
that handing them everything they want will achieve that goal.
Most of the parents we know feel the same way. Yet, most estate
plans are designed to give beneficiaries everything, with little or
no questions asked. Of course, there are a number of people who
put age limitations in their estate plans (for example, children
can receive trust assets at age 30). However, there is no particular
reason why giving the children a large amount of money at 30
will make them more self-reliant. Do you really want to send the
message that beneficiaries can stop work at 30 and live off their
inheritances?

How can you design your estate plan to ensure your heirs do
not become "trust fund babies"?

- Consider the type of behavior you want to reward. Is it public service? Is it holding down a full-time job? Is it being a
  full-time parent?

- What would be appropriate rewards or incentives for the
  behaviors you want to encourage? Some people suggest
  matching the earnings of the beneficiary; for example, if
  the beneficiary is making $60,000 per year, the trust will
  distribute to that beneficiary an identical amount. However,
  remember that there are differences in earnings among
  various jobs. An inner-city schoolteacher makes significantly less than a successful insurance salesperson. You
  might argue that the inner-city schoolteacher's job is more

socially valuable than the insurance salesperson's job. Why would you reward the insurance salesperson just because he or she earns more? What message would that send to the schoolteacher? Other people suggest setting a particular dollar amount as a distribution for any child with a full-time job. In these types of cases, you may want to consider whether a full-time parent qualifies as a full-time job. And what happens if someone is working part-time and going to school part-time? Is that person disqualified from receiving distributions? And does any type of job count? If your son the architect quits his "stressful" job and becomes the chief "fries chef" at McDonald's, does that qualify?

RENEE'S LETTER

Dear Mom,

I always appreciated what you did for me as I was growing up. You taught me that hard work never killed anyone. You made me work that part-time job while I was in high school, so I could buy my first car and pay my way through college. That's not to say I didn't always secretly hope you would just go out and pay for those things for me. Even back then, though, I knew it made me a stronger and better person. I knew that I was learning the things I needed to know if I was going to succeed in life. I have succeeded. Thank you for making that possible.

I have to admit, I have never figured out why you didn't do the same things for Chris as he was growing up. I know he was ten years younger and you had more money by then, but what you did for me worked, so I assumed you would have continued on that path. I don't think Chris ever held down a job in high school, and, of course, he didn't need to work his way through college because he dropped out during his first semester. He's 36 now, and until you died last year, did he ever live on his own for more than a couple of months? Did he ever even hold down a job for more than a couple of months? I always thought you enabled him to become "nothing" by giving him everything.

Things haven't changed since you died. Your trust allows each of us to receive distributions for our "support," but only after taking into consideration our other resources. What this has meant in reality is that I receive nothing from the trust, because I make enough to support myself and my family, and Chris gets a monthly allowance to support himself. He hasn't had a job in the last two months. He tells me he would rather wait to look for a job after summer ends, because he wouldn't have the opportunity to use his boat if he is working full-time.

I am not upset about not qualifying for distributions from your trust. I am not jealous that Chris is receiving distributions. I just think that it is sad that, as in life, you are enabling Chris to to do nothing with his life. It is not fair to him.

Love,

Renee

Obviously, not everyone is going to react the same way in response to inheriting wealth. Some people will keep working, and others will quit their jobs and live off their newfound money. The question is, How do you want your heirs to react in response to receiving their inheritances? You need to consider each beneficiary separately, as an individual. If I predecease my parents and leave them some money to live off in their later years, I will be happy that they no longer have to work. On the other hand, I am going to feel differently if my brother quits his job after receiving my money.

Encouraging Social Responsibility

It is often said that with age comes wisdom. Sometimes, though, you do not have the time to instill the wisdom in your loved ones that you would like. You can use your estate plan to teach those you love what you otherwise may not get the chance to teach them during your life. When I was growing up, my mother used to take me every Christmas to buy presents for members of our church who couldn't afford presents for their children. I now live near a shelter for abused children. When my children were younger, I would pack up some of their stuffed animals to send to the shelter. As they get older, I plan to take them along to drop off the animals. I want them to actively participate in helping other, less fortunate children. If you are not around to do these things, you can set up your estate plan to encourage this type of behavior. How you do this is limited only by your imagination. For example:

- Make annual distributions from your children's trusts to local shelters. This will, in essence, be a continuation of your packing up things that belong to them and delivering them to shelters. Even if your children don't want to give up their money (as they sometimes don't want to give up their stuffed animals), you will be teaching them an important lesson.

- Make distributions to your children contingent on their volunteering at children's shelters. This way your children have to demonstrate social responsibility as a condition of receiving your money.

- Put a stipulation in your estate plan that a certain amount of your money be held in trust for future distribution to various shelters with your children responsible for choosing the particular shelters. This will enable your children to be actively involved with the shelters.

Social responsibility need not be demonstrated so overtly.

ANNIE'S LETTER

Dear Dad,

I always thought that because I was a girl, you didn't think it was very important to teach me about money, investing, politics, or other traditionally male subjects. I don't think I even knew your party affiliation until I was in my early 30s. Looking back, I don't know that you would have taught a boy these things either.

I was surprised that you found a way to teach me about these things after you died. You must have given it a lot of thought while you were alive. It was such a small thing, but it spoke volumes to me. The only condition in my trust was that the funds be invested in stocks of companies that were not involved in any activities that damaged the environment. It really forced me to open my eyes about the environment—a cause, I will admit, I didn't spend much time thinking about.

I began researching companies, analyzing their operations, policies, and activities and started investing in the ones that met your criteria. I became aware of all of the companies that were polluting the environment and began to invest my nontrust monies much more prudently. It may have taken you a while, but thanks for the lesson, Dad. I have learned a lot.

Love,

Annie

It is not hard to provide your loved ones with guidance. It just takes time. Because you do not always know how much time you have, you need to make sure you use your estate plan to deliver to your loved ones the wisdom that you have acquired over the years.

5

Don't Let Your Emotions
Get the Better of You

PAUL'S LETTER

Dear Dad,

Since you have died, life has been . . . interesting. I thought you and I had done a good job getting your affairs in order before you died. Almost 94 years' worth of "stuff" is a lot to go through. It would have helped if you hadn't been such a saver. Do you remember how long it took us to organize those boxes of papers in the garage? I am still not sure why you needed to keep those cancelled checks from 1956.

I clearly remember the day we spent sorting through all of your "estate planning" documents. You had seven different wills and three different powers of attorney. We threw away everything except the copies with the latest dates, made an extra copy for me and another for Bob, and put them into separate three-ring binders.

You know Bob and I have always been close. But as brothers do sometimes, we got into a horrible fight this

year. It was over something stupid. Actually, it was between our wives, but we got trapped in the middle. When
you got sick, we put our hard feelings aside and both
worked together to make sure you got the best care. By the
time you died, our wives had resolved their differences,
and Bob and I were back to being friends.

Things were back to normal between us—until I went
through your three-ring binder. I could hardly believe
my eyes when I saw the new will. It didn't take long to
realize what had happened. Shortly after my disagree-
ment with Bob, he took you to a lawyer to change the executor of your will from me to the local bank. He and the
lawyer also changed the distributions, so that at either of
our deaths our share of your estate goes to the surviving
brother and not to our spouses. The truth is, I don't care
about not being the executor of your will. I do care, however, that Glenda cannot benefit from my share of your estate when I die.

Glenda and I have been married for 30 wonderful
years now. I could not imagine my life without my wife. I
am never going to have to imagine it now. A short time
before your death, I was diagnosed with liver cancer. I
didn't want to tell you with all that you had to deal with
yourself. The doctors have told me that I have less than
six months to live. I have already had to stop teaching.
Glenda has taken a leave from the school to help care for
me. I have provided for Glenda the best I can, but on a
teacher's salary we have not built up the kind of nest egg
I would have liked to leave her. The money from you
would certainly have gone a long way toward helping her
when I am gone.

I am sure you were emotional when you signed the
new will. I know Bob was emotional when he took you to
the lawyer. He has told me time and again how sorry he
is about the whole situation. I am not mad at him or at

you, Dad. I don't have time to be angry. Bob and I talked about making the new will "go away" and about going back to the old one. Unfortunately, the bank will not let us go forward with that plan. I only know that emotions shouldn't play such a large role in life (or death) decisions.

Your son,

Paul

Think before You Act

Families bring out the best and worst of our emotions. Child psychology books will tell you that children exhibit their worst behavior around their parents, because they know their parents will continue to love them anyway. And, we have all heard the terrible statistics about the overwhelming percentage of murders committed by family members. Family members, in fact, are often the first suspects when someone is abused or killed, because the emotions between family members are generally more volatile than with any others. When we let our emotions overcome our judgment, we often wind up with results that we hadn't intended. Had Paul's father been less emotional about Paul and Bob's fight, the consequences may have been very different. Running to the lawyer to fix your will each time your relationship with your child is strained will not only run up huge attorney's fees but also may be something you regret later. After you have calmed down, don't you find that things are not nearly as big of a deal as they originally seemed? Too many times, people do things based on emotions that they would regret if they were still alive to see the consequences. Paul's father would be one of them.

You need to think through the consequences of your actions. If Paul had predeceased his father, his father may have considered making Glenda a beneficiary of his estate. If he could have anticipated Paul's early death, he may not ever have made the change in the first place. Everything you do in your estate plan speaks volumes to the ones who remain and must live through its consequences.

DON'S STORY

I met Don before his wife died. Back then I guess you would call Don your typical workaholic. He worked 14-hour days, six days a week and sometimes on Sundays. I got the impression he had been that way from the time he and Angela married. I think as the kids were growing up, Angela took over the roles of both mother and father in the house. I don't mean to suggest that Don never saw his children, but I don't think he spent a lot of time tossing a baseball around in the front yard.

The kids were already grown and out of the house when Angela died. Her death really shook Don up. He started to slow down at work and eventually started dating. The kids were not too happy about the whole dating business. One evening they really let Don have it. As are typical of family fights, things were said that were best left unsaid. The kids went so far as to accuse Don of being a terrible father and an even worse husband to Angela. Don was so angry he kicked them out of his house and told them he never wanted to see them again.

After telling me the whole story, Don asked me for a recommendation for an attorney. He wanted to draft a will leaving all but 2 percent of his estate to his college. As a slap in the face, he would leave the remaining 2 percent to his children. As his accountant for several years, I knew he was talking about tens of millions of dollars. I tried to talk him into waiting until he could think more rationally about the situation. He would hear nothing of it. He told me that the sooner this was taken care of, the better. I sent him to a local attorney, who drafted a new will for him.

Almost a year later, Don told me that he and the kids had patched things up, and he wanted to make sure that he left them the bulk of his estate. He spoke of flipping around the percentages, so the kids would receive 98 percent of his estate and his college would receive 2 percent. Don was scheduled to meet with the lawyer the next week. He was frantic to get this fixed right away, just in case something happened to him.

A couple of weeks later, Don told me that he had been to the new lawyer and that he was going in to sign the new will the next day. He seemed to be much calmer than the last time I had seen him. That night, Don had a stroke. He died the next morning without ever regaining consciousness. He never had a chance to sign the new will.

I assumed that even though he had never signed the new will, Don had communicated his wishes to the lawyer, and his wishes would still be honored. I was wrong. Apparently, it is not enough to indicate your wishes to another individual, even a lawyer. You have to actually sign something to give effect to those wishes.

We tried to talk to the college about relinquishing its claim, but based on the numbers, it was unwilling to do so. In the end, the college received slightly less than $13 million, and the children received roughly $250,000 to be split between the four of them. Don's kids were left with virtually none of the money that he had spent their childhood earning. If he had only let some time pass before going to see the lawyer the first time, this might never have happened.

Words Once Spoken Are Hard to Retract

The problem with letting your emotions dictate the terms of your estate plan is that you may not be able to change the provisions in the future. Although most people's wills and trusts can be amended or revoked at any time, they become irrevocable when the person dies. If you have a change of heart based on a volatile, emotional event, you should try to carefully consider all of the consequences. Just because you want to write someone out of your will today may not mean you will want him or her out tomorrow. What happens if you make amends and do not have the time to fix your estate plan? That is exactly what happened to Don. He waited too long and wound up dying with a plan he no longer wanted.

If you are sure you want to make a change based on some emotional event, you may want to try putting your changes in writing first. Once you see the changes in writing, you have the option of ripping up the paper as soon as you read it. If you are still certain you want the changes included in your estate plan after writing them down, you can create an actual amendment to your trust or a codicil to your will. The steps necessary to formalize a change will vary from state to state. The benefit of preparing your own changes is that the changes are effective immediately without having to wait for an appointment with the attorney.

Also, if you have a change of heart, you will not feel obligated to sign the document just because you spent a lot of money having an attorney prepare the document. Eventually, you should have a lawyer draft the amendment or codicil, so you are sure that the changes actually reflect your intentions and are fully effective.

When you review your proposed changes, try to imagine various circumstances that might affect how you view your beneficiaries. For example, if you have disinherited your son because of some argument the two of you have had, how would you feel if he needed the money for some catastrophic medical emergency? Maybe that contingency should be drafted into your documents?

Will the changes inadvertently affect other people? For example, if your son is disinherited, won't that also affect your son's children? Just because you are mad at him does not mean you are necessarily mad at his children.

Assuming you have had time to calm down and still want to change your estate plan, you can call the attorney at that time to formalize the changes.

Once you are beyond the emotions and back to rational thinking, if you want your plan to contain provisions that disinherit a possible beneficiary or severely limit his or her access to your estate, you need to make sure you put some "teeth" into the plan. Although you may have rational reasons for doing whatever you decide to do, your beneficiary may not be all that rational when he or she discovers what you have done.

TRUDY'S STORY

Grace and I have been friends for 55 years. She was there for me when my husband and I divorced. I was with her at her husband Harold's bedside when he died. There wasn't anything we wouldn't do for each other.

After Harold died, Grace and her younger daughter had a falling out. I can remember finding Grace at home crying after more than one argument with Maggie. Eventually, Grace and Maggie stopped speaking altogether. As time passed, Grace made attempts to repair the relationship, but Maggie was not interested. On Grace's 75th birthday, she called Maggie, but Maggie's husband told Grace that Maggie couldn't come to the phone. He told her that he would have Maggie call her back. The call never came. Two days later, Grace was killed in a car accident. I was stunned.

A few days after the funeral, Grace's son Ben, her older daughter Judy, and I met with Grace's estate planning attorney. Grace had named me as the executor of her estate. I felt honored that she entrusted me with such a great responsibility. Grace left everything to Ben and Judy. She made no provisions for Maggie in her will. I was sorry to see that this was the last word on the issue, that Grace couldn't have put some of the hurt behind her and still treated Maggie equally with the other children. Sometimes, I think, family wounds are the hardest to repair.

However, Grace did not have the last word. About three weeks after Grace's funeral, I received a letter from Maggie's attorney. Maggie had decided to contest Grace's will. Because Grace had signed the will only three months before her death, Maggie claimed that Grace was incompetent at the time she signed the will. Incompetent! I could just see Grace turning over in her grave at that one!

The lawyers told me that the no contest provision in Grace's will was valid, but because Maggie was not a beneficiary, the provision had no "teeth" to it. It does no good to cut someone out of your will from which he or she wasn't going to inherit in the first place. Apparently, there is no disincentive not to contest.

Well, I did what I thought was right. I defended Grace's will for over a year. I read Maggie's depositions and the terrible things she said about Grace—much of which I knew wasn't true. I had to fight to uphold my friend's wishes. Ben and Judy eventually asked me to settle with Maggie. They wanted to support their mother's wishes, but the longer this thing dragged on, the more Grace's name was dragged through the mud. Then there was all the money we spent for lawyers. It was hard on all of us. Maggie, on the other hand, wasn't spending a penny on lawyer's fees. Her lawyer was working on a contingency fee basis. After a lot of haggling, Maggie finally agreed to settle for 25 percent of Grace's estate.

I am sorry if I let you down, Grace.

If You Mean It, Prove It

It does no good to disinherit someone who can then come back to sue your other heirs after your death. What can you do to protect your intended beneficiaries from your unintended beneficiaries?

- Have your lawyer draft no contest provisions into the documents. A no contest provision will state that a person who contests the provisions of the documents will automatically be disinherited. Some states allow the provisions to be even stricter and will disinherit the contestant as well as the contestant's descendants. A person might think twice about suing the estate if it means that not only is she at risk of losing her inheritance but so also are her children.

- Oftentimes, no contest provisions only mean something if the person contesting is a beneficiary of some sort. If I disinherit one of my daughters, and the penalty to contesting my estate plan is that she be disinherited, there is no disincentive for her if she contests. In a will (or trust) contest, the goal of the contestant is not necessarily to prevail at trial, it is to wear the other beneficiaries down until they are willing to settle. In Grace's case, if she had left something to Maggie, even if it was nominal compared to what the other children were getting, Maggie may have thought twice about filing the lawsuit. She may not have wanted to risk the amount she otherwise would be getting by having the no contest provision kick in.

Blinded by Love

When you think about which emotions can get the better of you, you typically think about negative emotions like jealousy and rage. We all know people who have been consumed by that passionate emotion on the other side of the spectrum—love. Have you ever seen an older gentleman with a cute young thing on his arm and wonder why he does not see that she is clearly after his money? That is what is called being blinded by love. Actions taken while under the influence of this emotion can result in some of the same dire consequences as those taken while blinded by rage. When you are planning for the loved ones in your life, don't let the all-consuming love for one put your planning at risk.

CHRISTINE'S STORY

Neil and I had been married seven years when he died. It was a second marriage for each of us. I was divorced, and Neil was a widower. We each had two grown children when we married, so we did not become the stereotypical blended family. We spent most of our holidays with Neil's kids and their families. My kids split holidays between our house and their father's house.

Neil had most of the money when we married, nearly $100,000. I had closer to $50,000, including the equity in my house. Over our seven-year marriage, our assets doubled in value. After so many years of marriage, I had really stopped looking at what we had together as his or mine. It was ours.

About five years into our marriage, we decided it was time to do our estate plan. We used a lawyer friend of Neil's to draft our living trust. I was concerned that if our marriage were to end, Neil might find someone new and leave everything to her. Neil wanted to leave a little bit directly to his children, but I didn't think that was appropriate, as I might need the money for my support. Clearly, if he loved me he would make sure I was provided for in the event something happened to him, just as I would for him if I died. In the end, we decided that each of us would leave everything to the survivor, and that the survivor would leave everything equally to all four children.

After what happened following Neil's death, there was just no way I could be comfortable with those provisions. Knowing how traumatic Neil's death was for me, his children could have been more supportive. They could have been more interested in how I was doing and more sympathetic to what I was going through.

I hired a new lawyer to amend the trust. Without Neil, I saw no reason to go back to his friend who prepared our original estate plan. I told the lawyer I wanted to change the provisions of the trust to leave everything to my two children only. He was very helpful. It's really too bad that Neil's children weren't there for me when I needed them.

When Neil and Christine met, Neil confided in some of his friends that he could not believe that someone like Christine would be interested in someone like him. Throughout their marriage, Neil's friends described him as smitten with Christine. When it came time for planning their estates, he had really wanted to make sure he left something for his children. After all, since their mother was already deceased, they had no one else who would be leaving them anything. Neil's daughter, in particular, could use the money, as her husband, a police officer, had recently been shot and killed in the line of duty, leaving her to raise their three young children alone. When Christine made clear that she thought that it was a sign of love that they leave everything to each other, he felt that he had no choice but to show her how much he loved her. It was not as though he did not trust her. They had, after all, agreed that they would each take care of each other's children after the second death.

Neil is a clear example of someone who is blinded by love. His intentions were good, and he did take care to have the trust drafted to go four ways after the second death. What Neil did not consider was how circumstances might influence Christine's intentions. There were no barriers preventing her from doing exactly what she did—disinheriting his children. Neil failed to see that circumstances could change in the future and put his children's inheritance at risk. What if in Christine's later years, a home health worker convinced Christine to leave all of the estate to her? What if Christine remarried someone who also felt that anything they owned was their joint property? What if Christine's children pressured her to make a change to the plan?

Although you certainly want your estate plan to reflect your feelings, you do not want to let it be driven by your emotions. Consider how your intentions could be annulled by the "emotional" provisions guiding your estate plan:

- If you leave everything to your spouse or significant other, will he or she ensure that your intended beneficiaries are the ultimate recipients of your estate? The last thing you want is a situation where the last one standing wins. When you leave everything you have to another, with nothing more than a promise that the assets will ultimately wind up in the right hands, you risk that promise not being kept (whether for malicious reasons or unforeseen life events).

- On the other hand, if you leave assets to someone other than your spouse or significant other, will that spouse or significant other be sufficiently provided for during his or her life? Try to think about what you would do with the money if you were still alive. If your spouse had health needs, would you refuse to pay for them, because you are saving money to give to your children? If you would pay for the health needs of your spouse while you are alive, why would that change at death?

- Have you made some improper assumptions? Just because you and your spouse have been married for 30 years and have no children from previous marriages does not mean that the survivor is automatically going to take care of your children at death. There is always the possibility that the survivor remarries, or that the survivor and the children grow distant. Maybe an in-law comes between the two of them (as some sons-in-law and daughters-in-law have been known to do).

Express Your Emotions, but Don't Be Ruled by Them

Not letting your emotions get the better of you when you prepare your estate plan does not mean that your emotions should not play a part in your estate planning. Estate planning is emotional. Most people are emotional about what happens after they die and for that reason prepare a plan to provide for those they love after they are gone. Make sure that you integrate your emotions appropriately into your estate plan. When you make emotional decisions in your estate plan, do not rely on the legalese of the documents to express how you really feel. Incorporate the emotional aspect of your plan into the language of the documents, just as you do for the financial part of your plan.

MAUREEN'S LETTER

Dear Rick,

When you died, I thought my life was over, too. I didn't know how I was going to continue without you. But as many people learn to do, I kept going one day at a time. It has been difficult and I still miss you desperately, but I am starting to live again. I think the greatest help in these awful months has been the support of your parents. With both of my parents and you gone, I had no one else. In the beginning, I wasn't sure how to react to them. I know they never approved of us living together. I never felt that they were very fond of me, either. I couldn't figure out why all of a sudden they were being so nice to me. I assumed that they were just reaching out to someone who had been close to you, trying to keep some of you alive.

Eventually, I learned that their concern was a result of your will. I never saw your will before you died. I actually never even knew you had one. Because I had a great deal of money as a result of my parents' deaths, I assumed that if you had done any planning, you wouldn't provide for me in your plan. How could I have been so wrong.

You were the most incredible man that has ever lived. I don't know what made you do what you did. By leaving all of your money to your parents and brothers, you ensured that there would be no animosity as a result of the money. But then, by telling them page after page of stories about our lives, our love, our thoughts, and our goals, you made them see me as you saw me. Because they could finally see why you loved me, they began to love me, too. You left me the one thing I needed the most—a family.

Thank you for giving me your family.

Love,

Maureen

The more you incorporate the feelings behind your estate planning decisions, the more likely you are to have a plan that reflects you, your values, and your ideals. And, the more likely it is to be a good plan. How can your child understand why you required he work 40 hours a week as a condition of his inheritance, unless you explain that you did not grow up until you started working? How can your parents understand that you chose your brother rather than them as the guardian for your children, unless you explain that you want them to be able to have a golden retirement, not one spent repeating their 30s with all the responsibilities of raising children? It is the detached plan, the one that lawyers draft by inserting your name into the blanks, that is a bad plan, not the one that warmly includes your emotions.

The trick is to let your feelings influence the design of your plan without letting your emotions get the better of you. It is not an easy balance, but once you have managed it, you will have a plan that is truly worthy of you and your loved ones.

6

How Much Is Enough?

EDNA'S LETTER

Dear Mom and Dad,

It was really hard on us kids losing you both at the same time. Maybe that is why Nicki and Art seemed to go a bit crazy after we finished probating your estates. At first, I didn't think much of it. Art bought a new convertible and a huge sailboat. But, when he took a "leave of absence" from his job and sailed the world on his new boat, I began to question his lifestyle. When he would drop into town from time to time, he would cruise the local strip and hop from club to club—only the "best" clubs, though.

Nicki became the girl that every guy could count on. That was after she and Sean divorced. Nicki said that Sean was too "boring" for her. One fellow she dated for a while wanted to open a little shop down by the water. I am not sure how much Nicki gave him, but I know it was enough to get the place opened. The shop was dedicated solely to selling wind chimes. I never figured out what the next guy did for a living. It seemed that every other week he and Nicki were running off to Atlantic City trying their "luck" at the various craps tables.

I never thought my brother and sister would act this way. Of course, we all knew you had done quite well, but it didn't occur to us that you could leave us so much money. With all of your charity work, I expected you would have left a large portion of your estates to charity. And, with the money in our trust funds from grandma and grandpa, it wasn't like we needed the money.

I am sure you didn't work all your lives just so we could sit back and waste your money. That is exactly what Nicki and Art did. It only took three years for them both to spend all of their money. I think about how horrified you would be if you knew how two responsible adults in their late 20s and early 30s began acting like little kids in a candy store. I guess once they saw the million dollars, they just couldn't help themselves.

I wish you had known in advance what was going to happen. I wish you had thought about what receiving a million dollars might do to us. I wish you had been here to see them after they had spent all of the money. It was as if the money had become their identity. When it was gone, they felt as if they were gone, too.

Art has gone back to work. He was so broke that he had to sell both the car and the boat. He has become a bitter man. Nicki is no longer as interesting to the con artists. Without the men swarming around her, Nicki started to feel like she was no longer worth anything. She had to be hospitalized last year after she swallowed a bottle of sleeping pills. She claims it was an accident, but I know better.

I appreciate that you left us everything. I think, though, that it would have been better for everyone if you had only left us enough to get started in life. I never thought I would say this, but I think you left us too much.

Love,

Edna

Are You Sure You Want to Leave Them Everything?

We have all heard stories of people who squander their inheritances, who become less responsible members of society as a result of a large increase in wealth. I remember my first job at a law firm. Virtually every new attorney rushed right out and bought a new BMW, Mercedes, or other luxury vehicle after getting a few-thousand-dollar signing bonus and a steady paycheck. Can you imagine what they would have done with $50,000, $100,000, or $1 million? For the most part, these were educated adults pushing age 30. What happens to the money when our heirs are not well educated, not self-motivated, and not quite mature adults? Just last week a friend was telling me about her neighbors' children. Both parents passed away within a couple weeks of each other, and the children, both in their mid-30s, spent the entire inheritance in less than 18 months.

Most people have a good idea who they want to name as their beneficiaries. Generally, parents will name children or grandchildren, and single people may name nieces and nephews, friends, or other relatives. Who they want to inherit their assets is the one thing people are typically sure about. Some people will name a charity or charities to receive a portion of their estates. However, I have never met anyone who directly named the government as the beneficiary of his or her estate plan. Most people try to find ways to avoid having the government take a portion of their estate at death. There are a variety of different estate planning techniques designed to reduce estate taxes. There is nothing wrong with trying to reduce the amount of estate taxes at your death. Obviously, if estate taxes are reduced, there is more money left to go to your heirs. The question is, What amount is enough to leave to your heirs and what amount may be too much?

Try to approach your decision about how much to leave by looking at what you have and then by looking at what amount you want to give:

- If your beneficiaries are young, you may need to leave more to ensure they are clothed, housed, and educated until a certain age. You may want to make sure that your money can take care of the same basic necessities you would provide if you were still here. If there is not enough to take care of those basic things, there is no need to ask further questions. If you don't know how much will be enough, you may want to leave more than is necessary just to be safe. There is no magic rule that says when beneficiaries reach a certain age they have to receive what is left.

- While you are alive, would you hand large amounts of money to your children at age 25, 30, or 40, just because they were 25, 30, or 40? Or are these ages when they should be on their own, learning to find their own way in the world? Presumably by these ages, your beneficiaries will have figured out how to provide their own basic living expenses. Maybe there is some amount you want to leave to take care of their wants or dreams. How do you decide how much is enough in this case?

- Do you support people or charities now? Ask yourself whether it is important for you to continue giving a particular amount after your death to those people or charities. Will the charity be able to do without your yearly contribution if you do not include them in your estate plan?

- How much is too much to leave to your heirs? What kind of effect do you think extra money will have on your heirs? Is

$500,000 a good amount to leave your 25-year-old, or will that amount be wasted on someone so young? What message are you sending your family or other beneficiaries with this kind of bequest? If there were no tax or other consequences, would you give your 25-year-old $500,000, because it would allow him or her to fulfill a want or dream?

By looking at how much you want to leave your heirs first, you will be in a good position to determine what you want to have happen with the rest of the money. For instance, by leaving money to others or to charity, you may leave your family with something more valuable than your money—the lesson of helping others.

Instilling a Value Greater Than Wealth

The question becomes, What is the best way to teach these lessons? My parents were always vocal about the benefit of a good education. As a young child, my parents took me with them on trips to poor Third World countries, where the education systems were sometimes nonexistent. My parents believed that education was the key to a large number of the problems facing those countries. As I saw and experienced how much the issue of education meant to them, it began to take on more meaning for me.

When my parents died, I took a portion of my inheritance and used it to set up a foundation in their names. My first project for the foundation was to set up a fund for the parents of young girls in Kenya. The fund was designed to ensure that young girls in Kenya could stay in school, rather than be sold into marriage as young as ten years old. Recently, my focus has shifted to the women of Afghanistan and the terrible conditions under which they live. I have spent a lot of time talking to my children about how these women are not permitted an education. I struggle to make them understand that the plight of these women and girls should be our fight. I strongly believe that we must help them in their fight for the right to receive an education. Because they live in a society in which they cannot speak, we must be their voice and speak for them.

I hope that by my example, my children will come to support this and other worthwhile causes. My goal is to encourage them to support these causes not simply philosophically but also by active participation. I hope to serve as a role model to them, as my parents did for me. It is not nearly as important for me to give my children every penny I have as it is to instill in them the value of using our "pennies" for those who need them.

I am not foolish enough to think that if I die and leave my children a significant amount of money—even if they don't receive it until age 30, 40, or even 50—they will think about taking that money and giving it to others. It takes time to instill our own values in our children. However, it is one thing to talk about leaving too much to your heirs and another thing to translate leaving the money elsewhere into a valuable life lesson for our loved ones.

GRANT'S STORY

My parents worked hard their whole lives to build our family business. Caroline and I spent so much time in the shop as kids, it was no wonder that we both decided to go into the family business after college. Caroline and I worked very hard at the shop. We put more hours in than any other employees, even though we were the bosses' kids.

Apart from the business, Mom and Dad spent a considerable amount of time and effort volunteering at the local art museum. They believed that the museum added a great deal of culture to the community, which was pretty important to them. I never really understood the importance of a bunch of paintings.

Dad died a few years before Mom. After his death, Mom spent more and more time at the museum and less and less time at the shop. Caroline and I basically ran the whole place. It was no surprise to us that when Mom died, she left us the shop. We had earned it after all those years.

We were surprised to find that Mom and Dad had left virtually everything else to the museum. How were Caroline and I supposed to run the business without any working capital? Even after all the time we had put in, we still had to work day and night to make the business profitable. And, it would have been nice to have a little extra for us, so we could enjoy some of the finer things in life, instead of more stupid paintings in some big empty building.

If all you do is choose a particular amount to leave to your children and leave the balance to charity, your children may not appreciate your generous gift to charity and it may discourage them from giving to charity in the future. Obviously, Grant's parents were unable to instill in him the same appreciation they had for fine works of art and the legacy they impart to the culture of a community.

Just leaving an outright bequest to charity is not the only way to support a worthy cause. Also, as is clear from Grant's story, such a gift may not encourage your family to continue giving. In fact, it may have the opposite effect. Another alternative may be to put conditions on the distributions to your heirs. The distributions to your children may involve them performing some sort of community service. For example, for every hour of community service a child performs, he or she will receive a $100 or some other distribution. Depending on the personalities of your beneficiaries, this type of "incentive" to do community service is either going to enhance the benefits of giving to charity or will result in them resenting charity altogether.

There is also room in this type of design for misinterpreta-
tion. What type of community service counts? Will donating old
used items from the house qualify, or does it have to be volunteer
work? Will you waive the requirement in the case of a hardship on
a child who is widowed and raising four children on her own? Do
your beneficiaries have to work at particular charities, or can they
choose their own charities? What if you pick Catholic Charities,
and your son converts to another faith and marries a woman of
that faith? Is your charity one that would be of interest to your
beneficiaries? What if your beneficiary's choice of a charity is of
questionable integrity? Because you know your beneficiaries best,
you need to tailor these decisions to them. Just keep in mind that
it isn't as simple as placing a community service requirement on
them.

Another way to leave your money for the use of charities is
through setting up a family foundation. Family foundations typically are administered by your children or other relatives, who are
responsible for selecting recipient charities and making the distributions. You can designate a particular group of charities (like
the Red Cross, the American Heart Association, and the Guide
Dogs of America) or a particular type of charity (like inner-city
youth programs or institutes devoted to cancer research), or you
can leave the choice of charities totally to the discretion of the
board of the foundation. You can have multiple members of the
board involved in the selection and distribution, so that any one
beneficiary cannot circumvent the rules. This allows family members to receive the benefit of providing for charities but does not
tie their own particular inheritances to such funds.

It is possible that, like outright distributions to charity, your
beneficiaries may never appreciate the lesson of giving that you
seek to impart. More often than not, it is a great way to get family
members involved in charitable giving and have the family name
live on through your charitable legacy.

ANDREW'S STORY

When my mother's lawyer first read the provisions of her trust, I was a bit disappointed. As an only child, I assumed that Mother would leave me the bulk of her estate. Of course, I would never begrudge her friends or more distant relatives any amounts she might leave them. But I was not expecting her to leave such a large sum to charity.

Growing up, Mother was always involved in some charitable activity or another. There was always some function she was attending or a meeting she was running. We often took weekend trips to the local children's hospital or women's shelter to drop off toys or clothes. To be honest, I felt like she had given enough to charity while she was alive.

Rather than leaving her money to a particular charity or two, Mother created a foundation in the Smith family name and left me in charge. I was not sure why she would put me in charge. I was sure she knew I did not have the same charitable leanings as she did. In fact, I did not have charitable leanings at all. I considered resigning as director of the foundation. If someone was going to be giving away Mother's money to others, why did it have to be me? The lawyers told me that if I acted as director, I could take a director's fee. I did not need the money, but it was an attractive thought to at least be able to direct some of that money my way.

Initially, the job was pretty simple. We had monthly board meetings and considered requests by charities for funds from the foundation. Mother's only direction with respect to distributions from the foundation was that they had to benefit organizations that helped women and/or children in need. Once we made our first few distribu-

tions, we began receiving more and more requests. I was
overwhelmed by the number and types of organizations
that were involved in helping women and children. There
were abuse shelters, children's shelters, groups that specialized in getting women off of welfare and back into the
working world, and children's hospitals. The list went on
and on.

We began visiting the various organizations, so we
could make more informed decisions regarding our distributions. At some of our stops, we would meet the women
and children who benefited from the funds received by
these organizations. Their stories were incredible.

I particularly remember a four-year-old girl we met
at a local children's hospital. Her name was Chelsea.
Chelsea had been seriously burned in a fire the previous
Christmas. Over half of her body was scarred from the
burns. Her family's insurance would not cover operations
designed to minimize the scarring and restore her previous features. The scar tissue from the burns was so bad,
she was unable to even smile. The insurance company
called the operations cosmetic and said the family would
have to pay for the operations out of their own pocket.
Chelsea's family could not afford the very costly operations. They applied to a nearby charity that pays for sur-
geries for burn victims. The charity, with funds received
from our foundation, was able to pay for young Chelsea's
operation.

When I first saw Chelsea, she was recovering from
surgery on her face. In fact, she was smiling. I have a four-
year-old myself, and I cannot imagine what it would be
like to not see her smile.

I was proud of the efforts of our family foundation
and the effect we were able to have on the women and children of our community. Somewhere in between the lawyer's office and my drive home from the hospital that day,

it became "our family" foundation, not Mother's foundation. I came to realize that Mother left me something far more valuable than her money. She left me with the ability to do something for others. I can never thank her enough.

Andrew was an adult when his mother died. Although she had exposed him to the numerous charitable works in which she was involved, he didn't develop the same values regarding charity. By leaving him with the tools to help others, Andrew's mother enabled him to have his own experience of charitable giving and share in the joy she felt in giving in this way.

You can also provide for charity without making the distribution immediately on your death. With young children or grandchildren, you may want to wait until after they are established to leave money to charity. Think of it this way: If you die leaving two young children, say, ages eight and ten, you do not know how much they will need growing up and getting through college. You may be reluctant to leave anything to charity at your death in this case, even though you have strong charitable inclinations. You may want to include a provision that says you will provide for all of their needs until your children turn 25. At age 25, assuming there is still money left, one-half of the balance would go to charity.

This is not a strategy to reduce estate taxes, although it could be designed as one. It does allow you to accomplish your goals of caring for your children when they need it and still leave money to charity after they are grown. By leaving money to your children in this way, you are able to teach them that you honor your personal responsibilities first and your social responsibilities next. And, you provide them with a guide to handling their own responsibilities as they mature.

Charity Begins at Home

When you read the papers and hear about ultrawealthy people who talk about not leaving too much to their heirs, they often talk about public charities as alternative beneficiaries. Sometimes, the people you most need to help are the people right in front of you. Often, the focus during the estate planning process is on your immediate family, your children and spouse, so that you forget about extended family or close friends. If you have left enough for your children, are their other people you need to think about? As we discussed earlier, you cannot rely on others to take care of those to whom you have a responsibility. Remember how Marco and Anthony abandoned their grandfather after their parents' deaths?

Sometimes, stories about people like Marco and Anthony can be attributed to immaturity. You may think you know your brothers and sisters well enough to know that they will take care of your aging mother if she needs it. But do you know their spouses well enough to be sure that is true? How about their spouses to come, the young girl your brother marries during his midlife crisis? Will she be willing to take care of your mother? Will your brother be able to stand up to her when the time comes? Do you know their financial situations? If you leave everything to your brother, assuming he will take care of your mother, and then his new young wife divorces him and takes the money, how will he be able to help your mother?

DIANE'S STORY

I always thought my brother spoiled his children. Jason and I did not have it easy growing up. Mother was always there for us, though. Daddy got sick when I was about 7 and Jason was 9. He couldn't work most of our teenage years. When I was 17, Daddy died. Even throughout that difficult time, Mother was there for us. She held down two jobs and helped put both Jason and I through college. I didn't care so much, but I know it was hard for Jason, never having any extra money to buy tickets to football games or take a girl out to a nice dinner. I think that is why, when he became successful, he gave his children everything they wanted.

I wish I could say that my nephews were good kids, but the truth was they were spoiled rotten. As they got older, they seemed to get worse. Jason was constantly getting them out of the various jams they seemed to get themselves into. I think the hardest thing for me to accept about them was how poorly they treated Mother. They would say and do things as if they thought they were better than her, as if she were low-class. I can assure you, even if my mother didn't have a lot of money, she was the last person in the world who could be called low-class. I don't know if Jason ever knew how his sons treated Mother. I doubt it, because I cannot imagine him putting up with that kind of behavior.

Jason was overly generous not only to his children but also to all of us. I went into social work after college, not a high-paying profession. Jason was always slipping me a little cash when he knew things were tight. He even helped me with the tuition for my children when it came time to send them to college. He always said that it was important to him to make sure his family was taken care of, just as Mother took care of us when we were growing up. He practically supported Mother.

Jason died much too young. He was only 62. He left everything to his sons (Jason had been divorced for about six years before he died). As close as I can tell, there was about $10 million left after all of the taxes were paid. At 28 and 30, those boys became multimillionaires. After Jason's death, Mother moved in with me. The last I heard, the boys were off traveling the world. Not one shred of Jason's generosity made it into those boys. I am sure Jason assumed that his sons would take care of Mother. Otherwise, I am sure he would have provided for her himself.

Even though Diane never mentions it, she also lost the benefit of Jason's generosity after his death. Things were not easy for her before, and with her mother now living with her, it became more difficult to make ends meet. If Jason's mother had predeceased him, Diane could still have used a bit of money to make ends meet. Even assuming that Jason's children were good kids and were willing to take care of their grandmother, what is the likelihood that they would have been willing to help their aunt? With today's mobile society and families living in different states and countries, most aunts and uncles do not have a lot of opportunities to get to know their nieces and nephews. A family reunion once a year would not have given Jason's children the ability to know their aunt or even to understand her situation. It is also quite possible that Jason would never have told them about his helping Diane. So, how could we expect them to continue his generosity?

Don't be fooled into thinking that your heirs may be different from Jason's children and that they will take care of your other family members. Just because you are inclined to help others in need, does not mean that the people you love feel the same way. Your children, brothers and sisters, and even your spouse may have very different feelings about providing for other family members who need financial help. Sometimes, you may have to show them the way.

LISA'S STORY

Noelle is probably the nicest lady I have ever met. When I first met her, she was already 93. She didn't look a day past 70 to me. She confessed once that one of her secrets to a long life was to give as much of herself as she could to others. She explained that when she gave of herself, others gave back. It was a wonderful circle of giving. I know Noelle didn't limit herself to only giving her time. She was famous for giving her money away to every child, grandchild, and great-grandchild in need. She was a very smart woman, too. She did not throw money at every relative who came knocking. She would always ask a number of questions to determine whether the person was truly in need. Those truly in need got help. Those looking for a handout were turned away.

Noelle thought it was important for family to take care of family through good and bad times alike. She had such a friendly manner about her that it was easy to listen to her "lectures" about taking care of family. You didn't even feel like you were being lectured to. And, her lessons stuck with you. I can't remember any one of her children, grandchildren, or great-grandchildren refusing to help another in need.

When I told Noelle how much I aspired to be like her, she laughed her wonderful, bright laugh and told me that she had done nothing but teach her family to be responsible first for themselves and then for one another. She also told me that she believed the job of teaching loved ones important lessons continued forever. I didn't know what that meant until after she died.

Even though Noelle was able to pass some valuable lessons to her family, not all of them were old enough to learn those lessons. She always said that she had too much money to leave it to certain individuals. For the youngest family members, she set up a trust to provide for their needs and the needs of every other family member. That meant little Megan's share could be used to pay for her education and also for her father's health needs. Kyle's share could provide for his braces and also for his aunt's new roof. She gave clear instructions as to when a person qualified to take money from the trust. She also made each of the little ones, as they got older, take turns acting as cotrustees. This allowed them to learn the lesson, firsthand, of helping their family members.

Eventually, the trust funds ran out. To this day, I still keep in contact with a number of Noelle's family members. And each one, even the ones too young to have known Noelle, takes personal responsibility for the needs of the others.

Whether at home or elsewhere, you have options available to you when you have too much to leave to particular individuals. By taking the opportunity to leave those excess funds in a way that is responsible to your family, your community, and your society, it is also a tremendous way of teaching your loved ones about the rewards of giving.

CHAPTER

7

Life's Not Fair

KEVIN'S STORY

She never could have done it without me. I was the one who did all of the work. I was the one who struggled to make the right decisions. That is how it has always been. When Barbara and I were growing up, I was the responsible one. I was the one everyone expected to do the right thing. She escaped from her problems and shied away from difficult choices. She always relied on others to do what she couldn't or wouldn't do herself.

When Mom died and left us as cotrustees of her trust, I'll admit I was hurt at first. I am the older child, and I have proven many times that I am capable of handling a lot of responsibility. Barbara has never proven herself capable of anything. We were going to have to make financial decisions that would impact Dad. How was Barbara going to be able to do that? I knew Mom just named Barbara as a cotrustee so that Barbara's feelings wouldn't be hurt. It really wasn't fair.

It wasn't as bad as I thought. As I suspected, within a couple of months Barbara was back to doing her own thing, and I was doing what I should have been doing from the beginning—handling things. The only problem was that I had to get Barbara's signature every time I needed to open an account, make a trade, or write a check. In the beginning, it was pretty simple. I would gather the items I needed her to sign and bring them to Dad's house each Sunday while she was visiting. After about six months, Barbara moved halfway across the country. Now she was not only disinterested, she also was far away.

Initially, I would send her the account statements. Eventually, I asked myself, What's the point? It's not like she was ever going to look at them. I thought if she really wanted them, she would ask for them. She never asked.

After some time, I started signing her name on the trust accounts. It made things so much easier. She had never given me any reason to think she would mind. I was totally shocked when she accused me of trying to cheat the trust. I am sure her husband had something to do with it. He has always taken too much interest in our family's financial affairs. I didn't do anything that wasn't in Dad's best interest—and in ours.

BARBARA'S STORY

Kevin has always had such a high opinion of himself. I am competent. I am responsible. I am caring. I could never understand why Kevin thought so little of me. Mom knew, though, how well I could handle things. That is why she put both Kevin and me in charge of her trust. She knew I could temper his headstrong ways. Personally, I think she would have only chosen me, except that Kevin was older and she didn't want to hurt his feelings. It really wasn't fair.

At first, I did a pretty good job. I reviewed all of the trust account statements and was involved in all trust transactions. After six months, my husband got a promotion that took us to another state. I thought I could still act as cotrustee. I would just have to be more creative to properly handle my duties by fax, by wire, or by overnight mail. How hard could it be?

The first month a statement didn't come, I just thought that Kevin forgot. It slipped my mind for the next few months. I was pretty busy after the move and getting the kids started in new schools. I eventually realized that I wasn't getting any of the statements. He was taking over, like he always did.

I called the brokerage firm, and they started sending me a copy of the statement directly. I was mad, but I knew he couldn't do anything without me. Sure, there were times that I didn't go over the statements with a fine-tooth comb. I had my family to take care of and my life to live, too.

Then one day, my husband asked me how the trust account was doing. He had been investing some of our money on his own and thought he could do as well for Mom's account as he was doing for ours. He was not convinced that Kevin's broker knew what he was doing. As I looked at the statements from the previous few months, I began to realize that transactions took place and withdrawals were made that I had not authorized. How did Kevin do it? When I called him to ask about it, he told me he had signed my name. He did it so he wouldn't have to bother me. Bother me?! How could I ever trust him again?

Siblings Fight, So Why Force
Them to Work Together?

Kevin and Barbara clearly did not see things from the same perspective. The only thing they seemed to agree on was that being forced to act together was not fair. I spend most of my time with my two young daughters explaining to them that life is not fair. When it is Rachel's birthday, Julia does not also get to have a party. When ice cream is scooped out of the container, it does not always fill the bowls the same. And, just because I love them equally does not mean that I do or should treat them equally. One is older, one is taller, one is more athletic, and one is more musical. I wouldn't sign them up for the same extracurricular activities today, and I wouldn't sign them up for the same trustee job tomorrow. And, by the way, my children fight. They fight over toys and computer games, over who is the neighbor girl's best friend, and over who just touched who. I hear the same thing from other parents, too. Siblings do not always get along. So, when people die and there is no one to hold together the family fabric, why do they force their children to work together?

People sometimes try too hard to make their estate plan "fair" or "equal." Is that the lesson that Kevin and Barbara's mother wanted to teach them—that everything in life should be fair or equal? Probably not. Sometimes, in an effort to spare their children's feelings, parents fail to look at their children honestly and make decisions based on real life. Instead, they treat very different children the same. By forcing Kevin and Barbara, who did not get along well as children, to work together, their mother set them up for failure and hard feelings. If she felt one was better suited for the job, she could have put him or her in charge and then explained in her estate plan the reasons for her decision. For example, Barbara was too busy with her young children to saddle her with the burden of also acting as cotrustee. Or, Kevin had an accounting degree and would be more experienced in dealing with the details of her trust.

One of the most common problems with an estate plan involves the selection of a trustee. Following are several important points you need to consider when choosing a trustee:

- If you name one or more of your children as executor of your will or trustee of your trust, how will that affect the rest of your family? Is the child or children you select the best equipped to handle the job? Or, were you just trying to be fair? Will your other children agree with your assessment? If you have two children acting as executor or trustee, do they get along? Will they be able to work together if asked? Who will arbitrate disputes? If you have more than two children acting as executor or trustee, how will this work mechanically? Will you need all three, four, or five signatures on every document?

- If your children are still young, have you picked the same person as trustee and as guardian? If not, will it be cumbersome for your guardian to go to your trustee to get money for your children when they need it? Do your guardian and trustee get along with each other? If you have picked the same person, do you realize that you have no checks and balances in place? Obviously, you won't choose to have your children live with someone you don't trust. However, that doesn't mean the person you have chosen to raise your children is a responsible money manager. My sister is my hands-down choice to raise my children, but she has no experience managing money. I worry that with too much money, she can be convinced to invest in some risky deals. If she is the trustee for my children's money and also their guardian, no one is watching over her to make sure she is investing properly. Instead, if I name my brother as trustee and my sister as guardian, my sister is there to stop my brother from investing in speculative ventures.

- Will an independent third party be a better solution? The most common objection to appointing a third party, such as a bank or a trust company, is that it will charge a fee to manage the estate. The typical fee will be roughly 1 percent of assets under management per year. In my experience, most individuals, particularly siblings and other relatives, charge a similar fee to act as trustee or executor. Do you know why? Because once the arguments start, the job becomes particularly unbearable and the individuals feel they are entitled to the fee. What happens when they take the fee? The arguments that justified the fee in the first place get even stronger when the beneficiaries discover that the trustee took a fee. Think how you would feel if your older or even your younger brother was named as the trustee instead of you. Then, imagine him adding insult to injury by taking a fee.

The Problem with Power

Don't fool yourself into thinking that your children, siblings, or other family members all get along, so this problem does not pertain to you. There is not a family out there that doesn't have its share of squabbles. By placing one or more of your family members in a position of power, you only exacerbate the problems. You may not always be aware of the hidden feelings of your loved ones. As your children get older, they may not come to you with each little thing their siblings have done to annoy them. However, that doesn't mean they aren't keeping score, even if only subconsciously. If you then name the sibling who has done the offending as your executor or trustee, you are sure to strike a raw nerve with the other sibling.

ANDREA'S STORY

I went with my mother when she first met with her lawyer about her estate plan. It was a pretty easy meeting, until we got to the part about naming the successor trustee of Mother's trust after she died. She said she wanted to name me as the trustee. But, she was worried how my sister, April, would react. April had always been the rebel of the family. While I went to college close to home and then went into my father's business, April traveled the world and lived in a semi-commune a couple of states away. When April got married, we found out afterwards. That's just how she was—she did things in her way and in her own time. When my father died a few years ago, Mother looked to me to help manage her affairs. April flew in for the funeral and flew back out the next day.

Mother's lawyer tried to talk her into naming a trust company as trustee. He said it would help preserve April's and my relationship. I thought that was ridiculous. Sure, April and I had different perspectives on life, but we didn't hate each other. I also thought it would be silly for us to pay an outside company to manage the estate when I could do it for free. The lawyer even suggested that the trustee fees were a reasonable amount to pay to have things taken care of by a neutral party. Neither Mother nor I was convinced. Instead, Mother added a provision saying that if April no longer lived out of state, we would be cotrustees. Mother knew how much April loved her home and assumed that she would not move. She also thought the provision would ensure April's feelings were not hurt, because it would look like she had named me only because I lived closer. We were so wrong. April was furious that I was named as the sole trustee. She even went so far as to make it appear she was no longer living out of state. Eventually, she gave up on that idea.

Things were up and down between us during the administration of the estate. Sometimes, April would seem to appreciate all of the work I was doing, and other times she would spend hours on the phone questioning each and every decision I made. Finally, I had had enough and decided I was going to take a fee for my work on behalf of the trust. When I told the lawyer, he told me it would only make April more angry. I was reluctant to go against my mother's wishes, but I decided that the hoops through which April was making me jump were ridiculous and that I was entitled to some compensation as a result.

The lawyer was right about April's reaction. She was furious. She started screaming at me and accusing me of planning this from the start. She said that the only reason she hadn't moved back home to act as cotrustee was because I convinced her that it wasn't in her best interest. She went so far as to threaten to sue me if I took a fee. In the end, there was nothing April could do about it. I took a very reasonable fee in light of the extra work I had to do to always satisfy April. I haven't heard from April since I sent her the last check from Mother's trust. In fact, April didn't even call my daughter on her last birthday, even though it had been an annual ritual of theirs for the past ten years.

APRIL'S STORY

I am the first to admit I am not a financial wizard. But, it doesn't take an expert to sell a few assets and distribute the proceeds. When I first learned that Mother had put Andrea in charge of her estate, I was a bit upset.

I thought it was something we both should have been doing. When I read Mother's trust, it was clear she did want
both of us in charge. She just thought it would be more
difficult if I was living far away. I tried to set up a tempo-
rary residence close to Mother's house, so I could act as
cotrustee with Andrea. Andrea didn't like that at all. She
told me she could handle everything, and she would keep
me apprised of what took place. She thought it was more
important that I was back home with my new husband. I
agreed.

Periodically, I would call Andrea and ask her how
things were going with Mother's estate. She always seemed
to get defensive whenever I called. I felt like she didn't
want me questioning any of her decisions. I wasn't actually
trying to question her; I was just trying to be informed.

Out of nowhere one day, Andrea told me she was going to take a trustee's fee for managing Mother's estate.
That really upset me. It didn't seem right for her to take
some of my inheritance and call it her trustee fee, especially after she had talked me out of being cotrustee. I
gave her an earful that night. It didn't matter to Andrea,
though. When I got the final distribution check, it had
been reduced by Andrea's trustee fee. I still get furious
just thinking about it. I haven't even been able to call Andrea's children on their birthdays in fear that she will answer and I won't be able to contain my anger.

Clearly, from April's perspective her mother had intended
for her to also act as a trustee. Andrea's taking a trustee fee was
inappropriate. From Andrea's perspective, she would not be in
this position if her mother had just done what she really wanted
and named Andrea as the sole trustee. Their mother, in an effort
to appear fair, put them in a situation that was ready primed for
conflict.

Choosing an independent party isn't a guarantee that your heirs are going to feel they are being treated fairly. When you look to outside trustees and executors, your family members will likely feel that you didn't trust them enough to give them the job. Maybe there is actually some truth to their feelings. But, if you name one sister over another or all three children jointly, one or more of them will still feel it's not fair. Life isn't fair, and neither will life be fair after your death. You need to make these decisions based on the best knowledge you have at the time and not on some notion that you need to treat everyone fairly.

Once you have sorted out who is going to be responsible for distributing your assets to your beneficiaries, you still need to determine how much each beneficiary will receive. Again, no matter what you do, it will not seem fair to everyone. The notion of fairness is relative to the person voicing the objection.

SCOTT'S LETTER

Dear Mom,

Thank you. I know you always tried to treat Gina and me equally. I can still remember stacking up our piles of toys after Christmas and comparing them; they were always the same. I wondered how you were going to deal with our different family situations. Of course, I expected that Gina and I would get equal amounts, but I was not sure what you were going to do about our children. I think you worked it out perfectly.

I understood that the typical way of setting up trusts is to pass the estate in equal shares to the children of siblings. Because I have three children and Gina only has one, in this arrangement my children would each receive one-third of my one-half share, and Gina's son would receive her entire half. I was grateful to see that you did not follow the traditional route. Now when I die, all four grandchildren will share equally in my one-half, and when Gina dies the same will happen.

Thank you. It means a lot to my children and to me.

Love,

Scott

GINA'S LETTER

Dear Mom,

I am shocked. You always tried to treat Scott and me equally. I can still remember going to the candy store, and if you didn't have a nickel for each of us, neither of us got any candy. You didn't let us buy one and split it, because you said it would never break evenly. I expected that equal treatment to be part of your estate as well. I still can't believe it wasn't.

My friend, who is a lawyer, told me that normally when a person sets up trusts for his or her children, each child's share ultimately passes to his or her own children. This would mean that Scott's one-half share of your estate would pass to his children at his death, and mine would pass to my son. I was dismayed to see that you did not follow the traditional route. Instead, you gave all four grandchildren equal shares after Scott and I each die. It doesn't seem right that Scott's family should benefit more, just because he chose to have more children than me.

You always were so good about trying to be fair in the past. It hurts me to know that my son will be penalized, simply because he doesn't have any siblings. Why did you do this?

Love,

Gina

Fair Isn't Equal and Equal Isn't Fair

Sometimes, you try to do the best you can, but no matter what you do, someone is going to be unhappy. In Scott and Gina's case, Gina felt that by treating all of the grandchildren equally, her son got the short end of the stick. On the other hand, if the grandchildren only inherited their parent's one-half share, Scott would not have been happy. And that is the problem. Fair isn't always equal, and equal isn't always fair.

When determining the appropriate amounts to leave to beneficiaries, think about the message your decisions leave. Are they the messages you intended? If not, is there a better way to leave your estate that will actually deliver the messages you intend? Think about the following issues when determining what and how much to leave to others:

- Does each person in a particular class of people receive the same amount? If you designate your three sisters and three brothers as your beneficiaries, do they split the money six ways? If two of your siblings are wealthy in their own right, you may want to split the money only between the four less wealthy siblings. Consider whether that will be construed as punishing those who have worked hard for their money and rewarding those who have not. Certainly, your sister who has run up tens of thousands of dollars in credit card bills needs the money more than your banker brother. But, have you actually helped your sister by simply giving her the money to pay off her debts?

- Where does the money go if your named beneficiaries are no longer alive? If you name your children and one child predeceases you, does his or her share go to his or her children? What if one child has six children, and the other has one child? Do you treat the grandchildren equally or each family group equally? If you have chosen your "then living brothers and sisters" as your beneficiaries, only the ones that are living will inherit. That means those beloved daughters of your recently deceased brother will inherit nothing from you.

- Are the provisions for distribution the same for each of your beneficiaries? If you have a son who has had a drug problem in the past (and you are not sure about his use now), do you put restrictions on his access to money? If your beneficiaries are different ages, when can they receive the money? If you decide that all beneficiaries inherit when the youngest turns 30, then some beneficiaries are going to be significantly older before they receive any of the money. It would be like saying that none of your children can get their driver's licenses until all of them are old enough to get their driver's licenses. On the other hand, if you decide that each beneficiary needs to be 30 before he or she can get the money, then some beneficiaries will have to wait longer than others. This can be a particular problem where your younger beneficiaries are more mature, and they have to wait simply because of an arbitrary age requirement.

ERIC'S STORY

When I got the call that Aunt Gail died, I started thinking back to the last time I had seen her. It was at least ten years earlier. Aunt Gail was my father's sister.

She was a buyer for a company in Hong Kong. She was what you would call a career woman. She never married or had kids and seemed to be happy focusing on her career. As we were growing up, she often brought back lots of trinkets for my cousins, my sisters, and me from her trips overseas. We always looked forward to those visits from "Aunty Gail."

The last time I saw her was at my high school graduation. She made a special trip back from Hong Kong just to be there for me. I was thrilled. Aunt Gail was a stickler about getting an education. She would always say, "You can make a lot of money during your life, but an education helps you make a lot of yourself." She gave me $1,000 for graduation and insisted that I use it for college in the fall. I did just as she asked.

Aunt Gail was not able to make it back for my college graduation, but she did send a warm note and another $1,000—"get on my feet" money, she called it. I wanted to continue my education and get a master's degree, but I just didn't have the money to do it. My parents worked hard for their money and agreed to help all of us with our bachelor's degrees, but they were not able to help us beyond that. I was pretty disappointed about being unable to continue my education, especially when I saw my cousins continue theirs. My father's brother paid for each of his children's education through their master's degrees, and for two of them through their doctorates. Uncle Charlie had done very well during his life and could afford the added tuition payments. I figured I would work for a few years and then go back for my master's. Because I couldn't continue my own education, I did the next best thing. I took a job as a teacher. I guess Aunt Gail's messages really stuck.

My father was the executor of Aunt Gail's estate. When he got home from his meeting with the lawyer, I knew something was wrong. Later that night, he called us all together for a family meeting. He explained that Aunt Gail had a pretty unique will, and he wanted to explain it to us. Apparently, Aunt Gail left her entire estate to all of her nieces and nephews. I couldn't believe it. Now I would be able to go back to school and to get my master's degree. The problem, according to Dad, was that she had put a stipulation on how the money was to be distributed.

There were eight of us nieces and nephews. She left 60 percent of her estate to the three nieces and nephew who had not yet graduated from college (two were actually still in high school). The money was to be used to pay for their college and postgraduate work for as long as they chose to be in school. After the last one completed his or her master's degree, any part of the 60 percent remaining would be distributed to them in varying percentages, depending upon how far they went in their education. She left another 25 percent of her estate to the two of Uncle Charlie's children who had gotten their doctorates. She said that they had proven to her that they valued education as much as she did and wanted to reward them for that. I figured that left the remaining 15 percent for my sister (who had graduated from college two years ago with her bachelor's degree and was now getting married), my cousin Chad (Uncle Charlie's only child to end his education after receiving his master's degree), and me. I figured that would still give me enough money to get that master's degree. I couldn't believe it when Dad told us that Chad got 10 percent, and my sister and I split the remaining 5 percent. Aunt Gail's reasoning was that she wanted to reward Chad for pursuing his master's degree, but not to the level of his brother and sister, who each had their doctorates. Because my sister and I did not pursue our educations beyond our bachelor's degrees, we ended up at the bottom of Aunt Gail's education ladder.

I was dumbstruck. Unlike Uncle Charlie's kids, who didn't even value the education he had paid for, I knew that I wanted more than anything to get my master's degree. I would already have my degree, if it wasn't for the money. It just isn't fair that Aunt Gail barely left me enough to pay for one semester, and I still am not going to be able to go to school.

CHAD'S STORY

Eric is such a whiner. All I have heard from him the past few years has been, "if my father had the money," "if I could have continued my education" if, if, if. The truth is, Eric could have gone on to get his master's degree, but he would have had to work or borrow the money to go. I recognize that I am lucky to have had parents who were able to support my educational endeavors, but I still had to work for my degrees. In fact, in some ways it would have been easier if my parents hadn't paid for my degrees. I might have chosen social services, instead of business administration, which is what my father wanted. In any event, I was the one who took the classes. I was the one who had to maintain a 3.7 grade point average or risk having my tuition money stopped. I was the one who jumped at the opportunity to continue my schooling.

Now Eric wants to complain that he isn't getting as much from Aunt Gail as the rest of us. I say it is his own fault. I don't complain about my siblings getting more than me because they got a doctorate and I didn't. I could have gone on in my schooling, but I chose to get a job instead. That is just the way things work. Maybe Aunt Gail knew that if Eric were really serious about getting his master's degree, he would have gotten it by now. It has been six years since he graduated from college after all.

At first I felt bad for Eric and his sister, but then I realized it was not my fault that Aunt Gail left them less than she left the rest of us. She was very clear as to her reasons. And while I may have been given more things in life than Eric, he needs to realize that not everything in life is going to be given to us— that life just isn't fair.

It's hard to know for sure whether Gail understood why Eric didn't get a more advanced degree. Maybe she did understand, and maybe she thought that Eric could have done something about it in the six years since he graduated from college. Maybe her lesson to Eric is that when you really want something, you may have to overcome obstacles that are in your way. Maybe the message you want to leave your loved ones is that they need to learn and grow from the unfairness they experience in life.

CHAPTER

8

But *My* Family Is Unique

BRENDA'S STORY

I don't think anyone would call my family typical. When I was 17, my older sister left home. I never knew why, but she refused to have anything to do with us after that. A couple of years later, my younger brother was diagnosed with schizophrenia. He was all right when he was taking his medication, but he was never able to take care of himself. He worked sporadic minimum wage jobs but had to rely on state aid to pay for his necessities. I helped him out financially when I could and worked with him on setting up a budget and paying his bills. I was glad I could be of some help to my brother.

When I was 40, my mother was diagnosed with dementia. The dementia quickly progressed. My father and I made the tough decision to put her in a round-the-clock care facility, after she was found walking down a busy street in her nightgown. The doctors told us she was not likely to have a normal life expectancy. I figured we probably only had five to ten more years with her. Then, when

I was 42, the unimaginable happened. I got a call that my father had had a heart attack and had died immediately. I never thought my dad would be the first to go, and certainly not so soon.

I flew back home to take care of things. I called a lawyer to ask what I was supposed to do first. He mentioned that I needed to look for a will. I had never seen one and was sure that my parents had never signed one. I went through all of the papers in my father's desk, but no will. At the funeral, I mentioned to one of my parents' former neighbors, Pat, that it didn't look like my parents had ever prepared wills. Pat had been a lawyer before he retired. He shook his head knowingly. A couple of days later, I received a copy of my parents' wills in the mail. Pat had sent them.

When I was about 25, Pat had drafted wills for my parents. Pat was a criminal attorney, not an estate planning attorney, but I guess my father must have thought he knew what he was doing. My father's will said that half of everything was to go to a trust for my mother, and the rest equally to the three of us children. My father had provisions regarding my brother's disability and had also put in some rather unique provisions about my sister's inheritance being contingent on her reestablishing a relationship with our family. Overall, it seemed like a fair and decent will.

Then I read the executor provisions. My mother, who barely recognized me at this point, was named as the executor, followed by Pat. After the time I spent helping my father with my mother's affairs, and the years I spent working with my brother, I could not imagine anyone but me handling things. I certainly could not imagine Dad's retired neighbor friend being able to manage our unique family situation. I figured all I had to do was ask Pat to let me handle things, that it would be much easier on him. I figured wrong.

After much arguing, persuading, and begging, Pat finally agreed to allow me to act as executor of Dad's estate. Of course, this did not come without conditions. I could act as executor and gather and value the assets, and deal with the banks and the courts. But, when the assets were to be finally distributed to the trusts for my mother, my brother, and my sister, and to me, he wanted to be trustee of the trusts. I thought that was a battle I would save for another day. At least I would be responsible for handling the day-to-day affairs of the estate. Once he saw how well I managed the estate, he would certainly turn over the management of the trusts to me.

Probate was much harder than I thought it would be. First, I had to find a way to give notice to my sister, since she was a named beneficiary of the will. I actually looked forward to having the opportunity to get to know my sister again. It had been way too long. I just wished it would be under better circumstances. I started with one or two names of people I thought my sister might still communicate with. After several calls, I found someone who had kept in touch with her. My sister's friend explained to me that my sister had died just a month earlier. I had been so close to finding her. And even though I had not seen her in over 20 years, I had hoped to see her again and felt like the rug had been pulled out from under me.

I encountered many hurdles over the year it took to administer my father's estate. I'll admit there were many days that I wanted to walk away from everything. In the end, I thought I did a pretty decent job of handling things. As it came time to close the probate, I spoke to Pat about the possibility of acting as trustee of the trusts for my brother and my mother. He turned me down flat. He said that he felt this was a commitment he made to my parents that he had to keep. He reminded me that he had been a lawyer for over 40 years and explained that he was best qualified to handle the administration of the trusts. I talked to my lawyer about going to court to have this provision overturned. After all, my father's will was over 20 years old. He couldn't have meant to have those provisions apply today. The lawyers told me that it would not be possible without Pat's consent.

It has been three years now since my father died. My mother is still alive. I see her often, but I wonder how often she actually sees me. I think she needs more attendants taking care of her. Pat says that he doesn't think paying for more attendants is financially prudent.

My brother calls me every week or so. He tells me that Pat says the trust should not pay for his dental bills, his grocery bills, and his other living expenses. I hang up the phone from these calls and cry. I have tried to talk to Pat about being more flexible with making payments to my brother. He just tries to put me off by saying that to ensure my brother continues to qualify for state aid, he needs to be very strict about any distributions. I have done a lot of investigating, and I don't think Pat needs to be so strict. But, he refuses to discuss my brother's trust with me anymore.

I wish I could have found a way to be the trustee. I wish I had been stronger with Pat from the beginning. I wish I could get Pat to listen to me now. I wish my father had updated his will when I was 30, 35, or 40.

If the lesson of Brenda's story were only that her parents should have updated their estate planning documents during the 20 years following their creation, her story would not be unique. Lots of people set up their estate plans and then forget all about them. The unique aspect of Brenda's story is that her brother had special needs as a result of his mental disability. Although her parents made sure to incorporate special language to cover his special needs, by failing to update their documents, they lost some of the effectiveness of the special needs provisions. Because Pat was not an estate planning attorney, he was not familiar enough with the rules for state aid to be able to effectively administer the trust. Brenda's brother may have been worse off under Pat's administration than he would have been if he had received the funds and lost the state aid.

The Special Challenges of Special Needs

It is often a challenge to properly plan for family members who have physical or psychological problems. Their needs are significantly different from the needs of others. They may need to be physically cared for their entire lives. They may not be able to handle their own financial affairs and may be receiving necessary state aid. Estate planning for such individuals typically call for "special needs" language—language that ensures their unique situations are dealt with on a very specialized basis, while still maintaining their ability to qualify for state aid.

To ensure the needs of special beneficiaries are properly met, you must answer several questions:

- Does the beneficiary qualify for state aid? If so, to continue qualifying for state aid, you will need to place restrictions on the access to the beneficiary's funds. You need to consider whether continued state aid justifies the restrictions on the funds you may want to leave to the beneficiary. Typically, the restrictions require that the funds you leave may only be used for the beneficiary's "special needs." The term "special needs" typically refers to items other than those that would be provided for by the state. For example, special needs could include distributions for vacations, but not for day-to-day medical expenses. The theory is that if the trust is designed to pay for those items that the state also covers, the trust should pay for those items first and the state should only make up any shortfall. For some, it may be worth losing the ability to receive the state support to be able to have the beneficiary have greater access to his or her inheritance.

• Does the beneficiary require a greater or lesser percentage of your estate? If your "special" beneficiary is receiving state aid and does not have a lot of "special needs," you may want to consider leaving him or her a smaller percentage of your estate. Otherwise, you will be leaving a significant amount in a trust that has restrictions on accessibility. If your other beneficiaries could use some of the funds, and your "special" beneficiary will be limited as to his or her access to the funds, you may want to alter the percentages among your beneficiaries.

• Can the beneficiary physically take care of himself or herself? If not, who is going to care for him or her after your death? Individuals with severe physical or mental disabilities may need a significant amount of attention by their caregivers. It is a difficult task to care for a disabled child. It is nearly an impossible task to find someone who can give the same level of care to your disabled adult child. Other children who have their own families and friends may not wish to take on such an obligation. Unlike naming a guardian for a minor child who only sees the child through age 18, the person who is responsible for a disabled beneficiary is taking on a duty for the rest of the beneficiary's life.

• Is your beneficiary able to handle his or her own financial affairs? If your "special" beneficiary is mentally competent, consider how the restrictions of a "special needs" trust will impact him or her. It is especially difficult for a physically disabled beneficiary to have significant restrictions placed on his or her trust but not on those of his or her siblings.

ED'S LETTER

Dear Mom,

I wanted you to know that I have been living on my own for the past three years. I have a part-time job doing computer work. I do most of my work from my house. I don't need to walk to be able to operate a computer from home. I hope eventually this will lead to a full-time job. Until then, I am relying on the money I get from the state to make ends meet.

I had hoped that I would be able to discontinue the state aid after you died. I figured the money I inherited would be enough to keep me going until I could fully support myself. I thought you understood this was my vision and hope for the future. Perhaps you didn't understand my vision and hope.

I am sure you thought you were doing the best thing for me by setting up a "special needs" trust for my inheritance. Unlike Janet and Doug, who received their inheritances immediately, I am unable to access my trust funds for even my most basic needs. Of course, this allows me to continue to qualify for state assistance, but Mom, I don't want to continue to qualify for state assistance. I want to be able to "stand" on my own.

Even worse, I have to go to Janet and Doug every time I want money from my trust. Frequently, they tell me that the request is denied, because it doesn't meet the strict guidelines set up by the trust. I know they are carrying out the terms of the trust, but I have to tell you, it doesn't make it any easier for me. I'm their older brother, but they treat me like a young child. I would have been happier going to a stranger to ask for money.

Plus, even though I know you did not intend it, I am humiliated. I am a grown man who simply happens to have a physical disability. I am not incompetent. I am not irresponsible. I am not a failure.

Love,

Ed

Most people focus on qualifying for state assistance when they create special needs trusts, but clearly there are times when qualifying for state assistance is of secondary importance to the other needs of the beneficiary. For Ed, to have had the opportunity to use his inheritance to help support himself would have meant much more than continuing to rely on the state for his support. Although Ed's mother clearly instilled in him the virtues of hard work and self-reliance when he was younger, she forgot to include those messages when she designed her estate plan. If they were important lessons to teach her young son, why weren't they important enough to include in her estate plan? With the best of intentions, Ed's mother lost sight of what was truly important to her and to her son.

No Two Families Are Alike

ANNA'S STORY

My mother and stepfather had been married for 12 years when he died. It was a second marriage for both of them. Joe had two children from his first marriage, and my mother had three. We were all teenagers when they got married. Joe's kids lived with their mother in the town next to ours.

Joe was quick to step into the role of being our father. It didn't take long before we felt as close to him as we did to our own father. Joe's daughters didn't feel quite the same way about my mother. Maybe it was because they didn't get the chance to live with her the way we did with Joe. Or maybe they resented Joe's new family and new life. Whatever the reason, they seemed to go out of their way to make my mother miserable when they were around. I know Joe must have seen it, but he never did anything about it. I always thought it was because he felt guilty he divorced their mother.

As they got older, Joe's daughters got a little bit better. They would never be best friends with my mother, but at least they were civil. In another ten years, I thought, they will be coming over for coffee in the afternoon. Unfortunately, we didn't have another ten years.

My mother called me at work the morning Joe died. She said he passed out at work and was being taken to the hospital. She asked me to call Joe's daughters and have them meet her at the hospital. I got in touch with Stacey. I had to leave a message for Elisa. By the time I got to the hospital, Joe was in surgery. He had an aneurysm and didn't make it through the surgery.

Stacey was shocked. She just walked aimlessly around the family waiting area as if she didn't know what else to do. I helped my mother fill out a bunch of paperwork and tried to comfort her as best I could. Elisa didn't show up at the hospital until nearly an hour later. She was furious we didn't try harder to reach her. I tried to explain that I called her on the only number I had, but she couldn't stop yelling. She blamed my mother for taking too long to call the ambulance, for not taking Joe to the other hospital in town (the "better" hospital), and for not giving me her work number so she could get here quicker. I am not sure what she thought she could have done if she had arrived while Joe was in surgery. I chalked up her behavior to the stress and circumstances of the moment and thought she would calm down after she got over the initial shock.

In the weeks following Joe's death, Elisa got worse. She insisted immediately on receiving a copy of Joe's trust, so she could take it to her own lawyer to review. She wanted us to know that she was going to ensure her rights were protected.

Joe left everything in trust for my mother. She would be entitled to live off his assets until her death. After her death, a small amount would be distributed to my brothers and me and the rest would go equally to Stacey and Elisa. My mother was named as the trustee of the trust.

From the time we read the trust, Elisa (and she got Stacey to join in, too) began harassing my mother about her management of the trust. They wanted accountings twice a year. They were constantly questioning her spending, even though she hardly took any money from the trust. They criticized her investment choices, saying that she should be more focused on growing the money for when they inherited it. We were back to how things were when Joe first married my mother. I wasn't surprised that all of the old hurts and jealousies had resurfaced.

I was always a little concerned about what would happen when Joe died. Even though Stacey and Elisa had become more civil towards my mother, it was clear they never thought of her as anything other than their father's wife. And frankly, Joe just never seemed to notice how they treated her. My poor mother was a wreck.

I've talked to my mother about letting someone else handle the trust. I thought Stacey and Elisa might be more tolerant if a third party were investing the money and making distributions to my mother. I didn't understand when my mother told me that involving a third party would just make things worse. I accused her of being stubborn and controlling, of not wanting to have to go to someone else to get distributions. I felt so ashamed when she showed me Joe's trust.

Joe clearly had never contemplated the problem my mother was facing. If she remained as trustee, Stacey and Elisa would make her life miserable. If she resigned as trustee, the successor trustee would take over the management of the trust. Stacey and Elisa were the successor cotrustees. By resigning, my mother would be jumping from the frying pan into the fire.

Most people are right when they say that their families are unique. It is never more true that no two families are alike than when it comes to blending two families together. It is hard enough to get natural siblings to blend together at times. But in the case of many second marriages, the parents' task is more difficult when some of the children live with the other parent.

Second marriages, whether there are children from both parents or only one parent, require a different approach to estate planning. The spouses need to focus on issues that typically do not come up when planning for the "traditional" family of father, mother, two kids, and a dog. When you are planning your estate in a second-marriage context, ask yourself whether your children from the prior relationship get along with your new spouse. If not, consider how to minimize any potential animosity between your children and your spouse. In a sole-marriage situation, one spouse generally allows the other spouse to use his or her assets until the second death and then have the remainder pass to the children. In the case of a second marriage, you may want to consider leaving some portion of your estate to your children immediately on your death. With an immediate distribution, the children will not be sitting around waiting (or wishing) for the death of your spouse. This could be especially important where your spouse is closer in age to your children than to you. If you truly want your children to inherit a portion of your estate, why make them wait until your spouse dies, especially if they are not particularly fond of him or her in the first place.

If you are concerned about not having enough money to support your spouse and to make a distribution to your children, consider alternatives like life insurance to fund a distribution to your children. If your children receive immediate cash at your death (from the insurance), and your spouse receives your other assets (or vice versa), you will likely reduce any friction as a result of your death. In fact, you could use the insurance as a substitute for leaving anything to your children after your spouse's death. This arrangement would further reduce possible hostilities by taking your children out of the position of being the overseer of your inheritance. If your children do not inherit until after your spouse dies, they are going to have a vested interest in seeing how your spouse is spending and investing the money, which is not a great position to be in if you are the surviving spouse or the children. By leaving some money directly to your children and other money directly to your spouse, you can avoid this problem. If Joe had left Stacey and Elisa some money at his death and everything else to his wife, Stacey and Elisa would not have been able to give his wife such a hard time.

When a second marriage occurs later in life, when the children are all adults, there may not be as much resentment of the new stepparent as when the children are younger. However, it may be more difficult to blend the two families into one. Even if the two parents come together to form their own family, it can be difficult to get the children from the two families to feel as if they all have a place in the new clan. Distance or the responsibilities of the children who have their own families and children may make the situation more difficult. If you are determined to make the two families a cohesive unit, find innovative ways to encourage family bonding.

When my husband and I married years ago, it was our intention to "bond" our new family of five young adults and teach them something important at the same time. We presented them with a challenge—each would each receive $4,000 to invest over a four-year period and whoever had the best returns at the end of each year would win a big prize. To make it even more interesting, whoever had the best overall performance at the end of the four years would win a round-the-world trip for two (economy class with our frequent-flier miles, of course). The rules were simple: They couldn't make loans or buy "things." They could get investment advice from each other, from brokers, or from us, but their investments had to be easy to value and their value easy to document. There was one additional requirement: Each year at a special family meeting, they would present their returns and what they had learned. It wasn't enough to be lucky with a stock and make a great return in a short period. The annual winner had to have a rational and repeatable investment strategy that he or she could explain to the others. We were amazed by what happened. Our children started talking to each other. They discussed strategies and asked each other for advice. One of my children and one of my husband's children actually pooled their money and invested it together, assuming this would cut down on transactional costs.

The annual family meetings were fun, and we were able to laugh at each other's mistakes and cheer for each other's successes. More important, family meetings were informative, because by requiring each of the children to speak before the others, they started to learn about each other, how they thought, what motivated them, and so on. The best part was that by structuring the experience as a game, none of the children looked at it as a way of being forced to become a family. It just happened naturally. And although they learned valuable lessons regarding investing, they learned the greatest lesson we could teach them— to appreciate the value of being a family.

KIM'S STORY

When my sister Robin met her husband Jason, she was 24 and he was 32. He had been married once before, briefly, and had a three-year-old daughter, Tiara. Tiara lived with her mother but spent a lot of time with Jason. When Robin and Jason married two years later, Tiara was clearly an important part of Robin's life. She loved Tiara as much as anyone.

Jason and Robin had two more children of their own, Jordan and Ally. When Tiara was 14, she came to live with Jason and Robin. Even though everything was fine with her own mother, she said she wanted to be part of the family together with Jordan and Ally. Her mother was from a wealthy family and traveled a lot. I got the feeling that Tiara really wanted to have a normal, stable life. She really did seem to fit in. She would help Ally with her homework and work with Jordan on his curve ball. Robin said they never had any problems with her throughout the four years she lived with them.

Robin and Jason were killed in an accident last year. Jordan is 15 and Ally is 12. I was named as their guardian in Robin and Jason's wills. Tiara came by to visit with them, but things changed after Robin and Jason died. Jason left his half of the estate equally to all three children, but Robin left her half of the estate to Jordan and Ally only. Tiara was devastated.

I know Tiara understood intellectually that she was not Robin's daughter. I also know that she didn't care so much about the money. She will have plenty of money from her mother and her mother's family. I think she felt part of the family and that Robin leaving her out of her will somehow made her feel she never really was a part of the family. I knew how much Robin loved Tiara, so I was surprised, too.

On my last visit to Robin and Jason's lawyer, I finally asked whether he knew why Robin did not include Tiara in her will. He explained to me that Robin was simply trying to ensure that her children were provided for in the event of her death. She knew that Tiara would never want for anything, because her natural mother could help her out when she needed it. Jordan and Ally only had Robin. If she didn't protect them financially, no one else would. He told me that Robin was very clear about her love for all three children, but she also knew that Tiara had someone else to care for her. As he explained it, Robin didn't equate the money with love; she was simply trying to be practical about the financial needs of all three children.

After the lawyer had explained it, everything made sense. I wanted to call Tiara right away and explain it to her. I knew she would see what a huge part of Robin's life she was. Over the years, Tiara had become such a big part of all of our lives. I never got the chance to make the call, because Tiara committed suicide that same day. She left a note saying, "I will never belong."

When you focus too much on one side of the family picture, it's possible to become blinded to the other side. If you only consider how your children interact with your spouse, you may miss any animosity among the stepchildren. If you focus solely on integrating both families, you may erase the unique qualities of each individual family. If you look at your estate plan only from your perspective, you run the risk of overlooking opportunities that may be more inclusive. If Robin had considered how Tiara might react to her will, she may have come up with a solution that met all of their needs. For example, she might have designed her will to provide for a single trust from which all three children would be entitled to take distributions based on need. Because Jordan and Ally clearly seemed to have a much greater financial need than Tiara, Tiara would have been unlikely to take distributions from the trust. However, she would have been treated as if she were an equal part of the family.

Every family is unique. Some families just have more exceptional circumstances than others. To ignore the special attributes of your family will only ensure that the lessons you may want to teach will never be learned.

9

Making Sure You Have Something to Leave

TIM'S STORY

Tim and Dawn are great people. All of their friends and neighbors speak very highly of them. Tim is a mechanical engineer for a local company, and Dawn works in one of the local high schools. They have twin five-year-old daughters they adore. Tim and Dawn first hired me as their financial planner shortly after their daughters were born. They did not have a lot of money to invest, but they wanted to set up educational funds for their daughters. I helped them set up a budget that would allow them to put away nearly $200 per month towards their daughters' educations. We invested the money wisely, and it has really started to grow. There is nearly $20,000 in the account now. Because their budget is so tight, we decided to invest the money in Tim and Dawn's names instead of in their daughters' names. This way, Tim and Dawn can get to the money if they ever need it for an emergency.

As part of our planning process, I reviewed Tim and Dawn's estate plan, their insurance coverage, and their retirement needs. On my advice, Tim and Dawn set up a will specifying who would care for their daughters if they died, increased Tim's life insurance coverage, and started making contributions to their companies' 401(k) plans. They really seemed to have their life together.

A couple of months ago, Tim was coming home from picking one of the girls up from soccer practice. A car in the lane next to him swerved into Tim's lane. Tim, in an effort to avoid a collision, swerved into the median. Tim and his daughter escaped with no injuries. Unfortunately, there was someone standing in the median waiting for traffic to clear so he could cross the street. By the time Tim saw the pedestrian, it was too late to avoid hitting him. The man suffered a fractured skull and was in a coma for nearly three weeks. According to the doctors, the man will have to go through extensive physical therapy, and there may be some permanent brain damage. Tim was horrified. Being the kind of person he is, Tim visited the man in the hospital several times.

When Tim told me the story, we immediately reviewed his insurance coverage to see how much his insurance would cover. Tim's policy limit on this type of incident was $250,000. Although we thought this was sufficient coverage before the accident, it turns out that $250,000 won't even cover the hospital costs. The man Tim hit had no health insurance, and the other driver was 21 with minimal coverage and no assets of his own.

Based on the lawsuit filed by the man's family, Tim and Dawn are going to lose most of their assets. The 401(k)s will be protected, as will a small amount of the equity in their home. Their savings accounts, brokerage account, and the account for their daughters will all go to pay any judgment. In hindsight, we probably should have done things differently. At a minimum, we could have put the education money into their daughters' names. Even if the money would not have been accessible to Tim and Dawn, it also would not have been subject to any judgments against them. Things are never as simple as they seem.

Why do you purchase homeowners insurance, car insurance, or fire insurance? Because it is protection against those unforeseen events that may cause you to lose your assets, those things you have worked hard to obtain —your cars, your home, and your savings. Purchasing insurance is an easy answer to simple problems. Life insurance will replace your future earnings in the event you die prematurely. But, what do you do if your problems are more complex and insurance won't help? How can you protect yourself from frivolous lawsuits or from life events that insurance won't cover? Remember, insurance companies are not in the business to pay every claim that comes across their desks. You may know someone who was in an accident or was liable for an incident at his or her home, and when that person tried to make a claim against the insurance company, all he or she encountered was red tape and no payment. To be safe, you need to find ways to protect your assets beyond simple insurance.

For some people, insurance coverage may be the asset protection vehicle of choice. It is simple, clean, cost effective, and generally sufficient to cover the risks of potential creditor claims. In theory, with enough insurance, your personal assets will not be at risk should you be sued. But, how much is enough insurance? Is $100,000 of collision coverage enough? What happens if the car you hit is carrying a surgeon who loses the use of his or her hands? That $100,000 may not even cover the loss of earnings for one year. Tim and Dawn—and even their advisor—thought that they had sufficient insurance to cover any incidents they might encounter. The problem is that you never know how much is enough.

You may ask, Why talk about protecting assets in a book about planning for what happens after death? First, unless you protect your assets during your life, how will you have anything to leave to your heirs? Second, many of the techniques available to protect your assets actually have their roots in estate planning. Third, by setting an example for your heirs by protecting what you have worked for, you may teach them to protect what you leave to them.

Weighing the Risk of Loss

The first thing you need to do when thinking about protecting your assets is to weigh the actual risk of losing them. To whom are you most likely to lose your assets? Are you a hairsbreadth away from an accident each time you get behind the wheel? Do you work in a profession where people are often sued? Are you a landlord or an employer? Do you live beyond your means? Certain people find themselves in situations that are breeding grounds for lawsuits. Others rarely find themselves in those situations.

I have a good friend who is an obstetrician. He is constantly being sued. Whenever a baby is born with some sort of complication or disorder, the doctor frequently is blamed. On the other hand, my sister designs PowerPoint presentations for her company. She doesn't supervise anyone and doesn't handle any of the money of the company. She doesn't even drive to work and instead takes the train. She makes a decent living and pays all of her bills. She does not have a high risk of being sued. Obviously, my doctor friend needs to be much more concerned about asset protection planning than my sister.

When it comes to deciding how much to protect their assets, my friend will go to greater lengths than my sister. In addition, the obstetrician has much more to protect than my sister. Does this mean that my sister should not do any asset protection planning? In fact, she may need to be more concerned about protecting what little she does have. If the doctor is sued for $100,000, he will likely be able to cover that bill. If my sister is sued for $100,000, it would wipe her out. She would lose her entire savings. Although it may seem more pressing for the doctor and may make sense for him to go to greater lengths to protect his assets, just because of the greater risk my sister still needs to make plans to protect her assets. How do you protect your assets? First you need to understand when and where you are vulnerable to attack.

Doubling the Risk with Joint Tenancy

Joint tenancy assets are extremely vulnerable assets. Why would joint tenancy make any difference in how easily a creditor can access your assets? The reason is that whenever you hold assets in joint tenancy, the assets are not only subject to the claims of your creditors but also to those of the other joint tenants.

MADELYNE'S LETTER

Dear Roger,

I dread writing this letter to you today. I know you haven't been well lately, and what I have to tell you may be quite a blow. Do you remember my business partner, Rex? Well, Rex was not the person I thought he was. Rex has been taking kickbacks from our customers under our government contracts. As a result, the government has stepped in and shut down our company. Even though I didn't know what Rex was doing, our business is set up so so that I am personally responsible for paying fines and other amounts. I wish I was telling you this because you are my brother and I need a shoulder to lean on. The truth is, you are going to be affected by this, too. Last year, we went to our lawyer and asked how you could avoid probate on your assets when you died. Do you remember what she told us? She said the best way to avoid probate was to create some sort of trust. You asked how much a trust would cost and whether there was a simpler (cheaper) way to avoid probate. She suggested putting your assets in joint tenancy with your heirs. When you added my name to your bank accounts, we agreed that I wouldn't take any of the money out of the accounts until your death. I didn't see this one coming. Now I have to tell you that not only won't I take any of the money out of your accounts, neither will you. The government has frozen all of my accounts, including those joint accounts. They are going to force me to use the money in those accounts to pay all that I owe, because my other assets are not enough to pay off the debts. I am so sorry, Roger. I never would have thought you would be penalized for something Rex did. I never thought I would be, either. I know you were counting on that money to take care of yourself as you got older. That just makes this letter even tougher to write. I will try to make it up to you—even if it takes me the rest of my life. I am so sorry.

Love,

Madelyne

Before he ever put Madelyne's name on his bank accounts, Roger did not have much in the way of an asset protection plan. When he added Madelyne's name to his accounts, his assets were even less protected. The minute someone else is listed jointly on your accounts, you have just inherited all of his or her past, present, and future problems. Joint tenancy makes you more vulnerable to creditor claims. Now, it may be possible for Roger to go to court and argue that the money is neither Madelyne's nor her creditor's to take. Even if he wins, which is highly unlikely, he will still have to pay lawyer's fees and other costs.

Obviously, when your intended heir is in a high-risk profession, carefully consider whether you want to add his or her name to your accounts as a joint tenant. Madelyne was not in a high-risk profession. At least, she didn't think she was, until she found out what Rex had done. Even if your personal risk of losing your assets in a lawsuit is relatively low, once you add another person or more people into the mix, your risk increases exponentially. Like Roger, you put your assets in greater jeopardy, just because you don't choose the appropriate strategy for your situation. Every strategy you encounter will have both pros and cons. The trick is to understand whether the pros (in Roger's case, the cheaper cost of joint tenancy over the cost of setting up a trust) outweigh the cons (the possible loss of assets to claims of Madelyne's creditors).

Assessing the Risk from Within

Even where you are not personally at high risk for a creditor claim and are not particularly vulnerable from an insurance or titling standpoint, you may be vulnerable from the one person who is supposed to protect you for life—your spouse. Even in today's society of second and third marriages, most spouses walk blindly into marriage when it comes to their assets. Marriages are supposed to be based on trust, and so we tend to leave ourselves vulnerable to our mates in matters of money. This is not to say we should be hoarding all of our assets in separate accounts. But, we need to be more aware of the risks involved regarding

creditors' rights if our spouses are sued. Remember the story of
Tim and Dawn? Tim was the one involved in the car accident,
which was not his fault, but the lawsuit will result in both Tim
and Dawn losing the assets for which they have worked so hard.

Of particular concern for many spouses is acquiring debt.
When you purchased your house, whose name was on the mortgage? Generally, it is both names, which means you are both
responsible for paying the mortgage. Depending on the state you
live in, you may be responsible for the mortgage even if you do
not sign the mortgage papers. Credit cards are another issue.
Under certain circumstances, and again depending on which
state you call home, credit card companies will look to either
spouse for payment. You will not be able to use your individuality
as a shield to protect you when creditors come calling. When you
promise to love, honor, and cherish, you often are also promising
to pay each other's debts.

Depending on the extent of your risk, your tolerance for ex-
posure, and the amount you are willing to pay to obtain creditor
protection, several strategies offer greater asset protection. Asset
protection should be thought of as a continuum of techniques
that ranges from the simple to the very complex. As we explained
earlier, every asset protection strategy has to be weighed against
the cons associated with the strategy. Not every strategy will be
right for you or even work for you.

Every state has laws on the books designed to protect creditors. The purpose of the laws is to ensure that creditors are not
swindled by debtors. Specifically, these laws say that individuals
cannot take steps designed to hinder, delay, or defraud creditors.
A strategy that is designed solely to make it difficult for someone
to sue you will be ignored, and the creditor will be able to access
your "protected" assets. As long as there are legitimate reasons
for the strategy, apart from creditor protection, the courts will
generally not allow the creditor to access the "protected" assets.

Hide the Money with the Kids

One of the most common asset protection strategies is to transfer assets to other family members. From the time your children are born, you are constantly shifting assets to them. You buy them bikes and pay for their school clothes. As they grow, you may help them with college tuition or to make the down payment on a first home. It is a natural progression to transfer your assets to your children. Many people consider transferring assets to their children when the possibility of a lawsuit is looming. If your assets are in your children's names, they will not be subject to creditors' claims, right? Wrong. Your assets may be subject to creditor claims, even if they are in the names of your children.

First, if you have made transfers to your children for no legitimate reason (e.g., you are not helping them pay for college or the transfer is not part of your estate plan), the transfers will be voided by a court. Just because you made the transfer to your children does not mean that the transfer will be considered valid. Isabel found this out the hard way.

ISABEL'S STORY

I had been a live-in day care giver to an elderly lady, Rose, for roughly 15 years before she died. I felt I had become part of Rose's family during that time. Obviously, she felt the same way, because she left me a percentage of her estate when she died. I was overwhelmed by her generosity. I had been a single mother from the time my children were young. It had always been a struggle to make ends meet. My children both got part-time jobs in high school, so they could start saving for college. When Rose died, I felt I could finally give my children the one thing I could never have afforded before—a decent college education.

I never expected the will to be contested. Rose's niece and nephew from back East tried to overturn the will, saying that I had coerced Rose into signing it. I didn't even know about the will until Rose died. When they saw that the coercion argument was not working, they accused me of stealing from Rose while she was alive! I'll admit that I was authorized to sign Rose's checks, but I only paid her bills. There also were a few times when I reimbursed myself for things I bought for Rose on my way into work., I always showed Rose the receipts and the checks that I wrote to myself. I guess I should have kept all those receipts over the years. The niece and nephew used the cancelled checks as evidence to show that I had been stealing from Rose. Not only were they trying to keep me from getting the money Rose left to me, but they also wanted me to pay back the estate the money they accused me of stealing!

I tried to get a lawyer to defend me, but I couldn't afford the several thousand dollars they asked as a retainer. I basically gave up on the idea of getting any of the inheritance. I figured that by settling with the niece and nephew regarding the inheritance, they would drop the lawsuit. Boy, was I wrong! Even after I agreed to give up the inheritance, they continued to fight me for the return of the other money. Of course, after all this time I had nothing to prove that these checks were reimbursement for Rose's expenses I had paid out of my own pocket.

I started asking my friends and neighbors how I could protect what little savings I had, about $16,000, from these greedy people. Some of them suggested I put the savings account in my children's names. It sounded like a good idea. After all, my kids needed the money for college (even though we privately agreed they wouldn't use it for college and would give it back when the lawsuit was over). I thought I had found the answer to my prayers. The judge didn't agree. He said that transferring assets to my children was an "act of defrauding" the niece and nephew. He said that with only $16,000 in savings and no other assets, I clearly was not in the position to be paying for my children's college. He also said that because I had not paid for any of their other years of college, it was clear this was only an attempt to get the assets out of my name. He ordered my children to turn the money over to the niece and nephew and then cited me for fraud. All I was trying to do was protect what was rightfully mine.

Second, even if your assets will be protected from the claims of your creditors, as is the case with joint tenancy assets, they will not be protected from the claims of your children's creditors. And, remember that creditors come in many shapes, sizes, and colors.

MATTHEW'S LETTER

Dear Mom and Dad,

I have been sitting here for hours trying to think how to tell you this: Cheryl left me. I guess I should have seen it coming. She has been complaining for months about how unhappy she has been. I thought she was just going through a tough time with the new baby and keeping up with our other two kids. It turns out the problem was me. After 15 years together, she says I don't give her enough attention. She says that I am spending too much time at work and not enough time with her. Even though I tell her all the time how much I love her, she says she needs someone who makes her feel *special*. Apparently, she found someone who makes her feel special. She moved out about two weeks ago, and moved in with a guy she met at the gym. She had already gone to a lawyer, and I was formally served with the divorce papers last week.

As if this isn't bad enough, Cheryl's lawyer has had all of our accounts frozen and wants 50 percent of each account. She is even asking for 50 percent of the account with money you asked me to hold for you while your dispute with your tenants was ongoing. I tried to talk to her about the account this afternoon, but she says the account has both of our names on it, and so half of it is hers. I saw a lawyer this morning who says it looks like she will be able to get everything she is asking for. I explained about the account, but he said that by holding the money in a bank account with Cheryl's name on it, I had effectively made half of it hers. I am at a loss.

I know this is the easy way out—writing you instead of calling you—but I just couldn't face you yet. I will certainly fight for the money, but the lawyer says it is a losing battle. I'm sorry. I never realized I was jeopardizing your money by putting it in a joint account with my wife! I am going to call her again and see if I can reason with her. I will keep you informed of my progress.

Your son,

Matthew

Third, even if assets are protected from the claims of your creditors and the claims of your children's creditors, they are still accessible by your children at any time. Most people respond to this statement by saying, "My children won't touch the money if I ask them not to." In most cases, this is true. But, things have a way of happening that you cannot predict. If a child loses a job, becomes involved with drugs or some other vice, is being pressured from a spouse, he or she may dip into the money with every intention of paying it back.

"Trust" the Tax Laws to Protect You

An alternative asset protection strategy is the use of trusts. Even though a typical revocable living trust does not give the person creating the trust any asset protection, there are several ways trusts can be used to protect assets. The rules about transfers in trust are the same as those for outright transfers. You cannot make transfers without an obvious purpose that does not include hindering, delaying, or defrauding your creditors. Generally, trusts are used for asset protection planning where you have a need to reduce the size of your estate for estate tax purposes.

It is not necessary here to describe each of these trusts in detail. What is important to remember with each of these trusts is that the trust's success as an asset protection vehicle is dependent on its necessity as an estate tax technique. For example, if your entire estate including your house is worth $750,000, there is no estate tax advantage to creating one of these trusts. Your estate is under the limit for estate taxes, and, therefore, the trust is not needed to reduce the size of your estate. If you do not have a need to reduce the size of your estate from an estate tax perspective, a transfer to one of these trusts could be ignored by a court, in the same way a transfer to your children might be.

Another important thing to remember about using a trust for asset protection planning is that these trusts generally must be irrevocable. Once you have created the trust, you cannot change it. When you have young heirs, it may be particularly important to maintain some flexibility in the terms of the trust.

Covering Yourself with Your Company

One final asset protection strategy is to create a corporation, partnership, or limited liability company and then to transfer your assets into that business entity. One of my biggest pet peeves involves lawyers and other advisors who go out and hawk partnerships, limited liability companies, and corporations as the panacea to all of your asset protection worries. There is no solution that is absolutely foolproof, and using business entities as your sole method of asset protection is a grievous mistake. Just as with the other asset protection strategies, consider the pros and cons of the use of business entities as an asset protection strategy.

PAT'S STORY

I have always been a very meticulous person. That trait has served me well as a doctor. I have always been concerned about liability. Face it, I am in a very vulnerable occupation when it comes to lawsuits. I have the maximum amount of insurance coverage, but I have two colleagues who recently lost cases against them for amounts greater than their insurance policy limits. I do not want to go through the same thing.

I read a number of books and articles on asset protection. I also went to several seminars on asset protection. Once I felt I had most of the information I needed to know, I went to a lawyer. The lawyer was one of the seminar presenters. He told me that the smartest thing I could do was to set up a series of limited liability companies.

Each limited liability company would hold a few of my assets. I would have one for my house, one for my art collection, one for my rental property, and one for my stocks and bonds. The lawyer told me that the limited liability companies would keep my assets protected, if I were sued for medical malpractice. He said I needed more than one, because if someone slipped and fell on my rental property, the most they could get was the rental property, because it was separated from the other assets.

When I was sued for malpractice last year, I thought I was protected. After I set up the limited liability companies, I reduced the amount of my malpractice insurance coverage. It was getting to be so expensive, and I was beginning to think I would have to quit my practice altogether. With my lower limits, my malpractice insurance did not cover the full amount the patient wanted. I knew I was fine, because I had those limited liability companies.

I couldn't believe my ears when the judge said that all except one of the limited liability companies were to be disregarded! He said that I clearly set them up to shield my assets from creditors. Of course I set them up to protect my assets. Why else would I pay for four limited liability companies? He said that to qualify for protection, each had to have a legitimate business purpose. He also said that he could think of no legitimate business purpose for a limited liability company to hold my artwork, my house, or my stocks and bonds. The only limited liability company he left intact was the one holding my rental property, because there could be legitimate business reasons for holding property in a business-type entity. He also told me that any good lawyer could have told me the same information. I guess the key words here are "good lawyer."

I lost almost everything. Having also to pay for the creation and maintenance of four limited liability companies only added injury to insult. I might have kept my malpractice insurance at a higher level or continued looking for a better avenue to protect my assets.

Unless there is a legitimate purpose for establishing a business entity, you are not likely to receive the creditor protection benefits associated with that type of entity. Pat quickly learned that lesson. Legitimate purposes need not always be business related, however. It may be that you want to transfer several pieces of property to an entity to consolidate the management of those properties. That would be a legitimate purpose. Or, you may want to transfer several assets to an entity, so you can start gifting interests to your family. There can be significant estate tax benefits associated with gifts of interests in business entities. Estate tax planning would be a legitimate purpose. Protecting your assets from present or future creditors is *not* a legitimate purpose. When designed properly and for the right purposes, business entities can provide significant protections.

NICK'S STORY

We moved around a lot when I was growing up. My father was in the Navy, so we were constantly being shipped from one place to another. I used to think of myself as a nomad wandering the desert looking for my home. I must have been about 12 when I first realized that some people actually owned their own homes. Ever since then, I have been obsessed with owning property.

I bought my first house, a small fixer-upper, when I was 26. By the time I was 35, I was renting that first house and owned three other rentals. I also had my own house and a small condominium I used on weekends. I finally achieved my dream. With the rents I was collecting on the four properties, I was able to build quite a nest egg.

Maybe because I was so obsessed with obtaining property, I was also very concerned about losing it. Actually, I could have lived through losing any or all of the rental properties, but not my home. I had finally established some roots, and I couldn't imagine ever having to move. I had plenty of insurance, so I figured I was covered in the event of most catastrophes I was still plagued by fears, however. I was particularly concerned about one of my properties that was in a bad neighborhood. I didn't even want to imagine what kinds of things could be going on there. I only knew for sure that if something went wrong, there was no amount of insurance that would protect me.

I had lots of friends who offered lots of advice regarding how to best protect myself and my assets. I finally went to a lawyer, who suggested that I set up two limited partnerships and a corporation. The partnerships would each hold two of my rentals. The corporation would be the general partner and consolidate the management of the properties inside the partnerships.

Late last year, the problem property burned down, and two of the tenants died. Apparently, one of the tenant's kids was in a gang and had angered a rival gang. They set fire to the house in the middle of the night. Even though the fire was clearly determined to be arson, the families of the two tenants filed a wrongful death suit against me. They said the materials I used to remodel the house before they moved in were no good and contributed to the speed at which the house burned down. They said that had I used slower-to-burn materials, the two deceased tenants would have had enough time to get out of the house. A jury agreed with them and awarded them a substantial sum. When I first heard the amount, I immediately began to think about my house. There was no way I could satisfy the judgment unless I sold my house—the last thing on Earth I wanted to do.

I didn't have to worry. The limited partnership and corporation protected most of my assets from attachment by the families. They were limited to collecting the

assets of the partnership—the land on which the burned
house once stood and the other rental property in that
partnership. Everything else was protected. I didn't have
to sell my house. I didn't have to uproot my family. I
didn't have to go back to being a nomad.

You may spend so much time thinking about how you are
going to pass your assets to your loved ones, you forget what
exactly it is you are going to pass to them. If you don't take the
time to protect what you've got, there may be nothing there to
pass. It is one thing to do as the bumper sticker instructed you
and "spend your children's inheritance." It is another thing
entirely if someone else stepped in and took it from you.

10

It's Not Just about the Money

JACK'S LETTER

Dear Dad,

We buried you last month. Well, I didn't. I went to the funeral but not to the grave site. I won't be coming to visit you there, either. You couldn't really expect me to be such a hypocrite.

I should have seen it coming. You were clear enough about your wishes when you were alive—after your death, have a family-only funeral and then ship your body back to Pennsylvania to be buried next to Mom. There was only one problem. When you married that other woman, you gave her all of the power.

Didn't you realize she would never let you be buried next to Mom? That this was an "insult" she would not bear? We were a close family before she came along. We all knew Mom's death hit you hard, but we didn't begrudge you for remarrying, even though we all knew it was on the rebound. We also knew you regretted your decision almost from the moment you made it. We also knew you were a man who would live by your vows. That was one of the things we respected most about you.

I still remember the last time I visited you. After she went upstairs to bed, you talked to me about how much you still missed Mom. I think it was the first time I had ever seen you cry. It wasn't until then that I realized how hard your life must have been since Mom's death.

You left no health care directives, no powers of attorney, and no directions in your will regarding your burial. This meant she was entitled to make all of the arrangements. Even though we are your flesh and blood, the law was on her side. We tried to reason with her. We explained that there was already a plot purchased next to Mom's. We even offered to pay for everything out of our own pockets. She was adamant that she would not be embarrassed in front of your friends and neighbors by having you buried next to Mom.

Your funeral was a large affair, with dozens of her friends from the "club." After the funeral, I skipped the graveside ceremony. I took the first flight home. Last week, Jim, Al, Ellen, Cathy, and I went to Mom's grave site. We said our good-byes to you there. And, that is where we will go when we want to visit with you.

Love,

Jack

Who Can You Count On to Abide by Your Wishes?

Family relations are probably the largest and least discussed part of estate planning. There is much more to the planning process than just what happens to the money. Maybe it is easier to think of estate planning in terms of passing wealth, rather than looking at it from the more personal side. In today's society, where the "traditional" family is no longer so traditional, it is even more important to make sure that you have taken care of the personal side of estate planning.

Jack's father knew from the time he married his second wife that his children didn't like her. In fact, the feelings were mutual. Initially, he thought things would change after they all got to know each other better. He was right—things got worse over time. Actually, Jack's father even began to regret his decision to marry so hastily after his first wife died, but he did not believe in divorce. His first wife, according to everyone who knew her, was the salt of the earth. He believed that he belonged with his first wife at death. He had been married to her for nearly 40 years. He explained to his second wife that there was already a plot purchased next to his first wife and that he felt it would be more appropriate to be buried along with other members of his family. He had even offered to purchase another plot in the same cemetery for her. He later told friends that she seemed agreeable to the arrangement.

Without any formal directions in a health care directive, will, or other similar document, his second wife was entitled to make any arrangements she wanted regarding his burial. It is important to have your wishes clearly spelled out, so no one can change them after you are gone. You should give instructions regarding burial, cremation, organ donation, and particularly life support. You've seen the television movies about fights between family members when a loved one is on life support. Each person seems to think that the person on life support would have chosen the option in which he himself is in favor. Remember, the only one who can speak for you after you are gone is you, so don't lose that voice by not indicating your wishes in your estate plan.

MARGARET'S STORY

My grandmother and her husband, Earl, had been married for almost 15 years when they separated. I am not sure who initiated the separation, but it was not an amicable separation for either of them. Earl moved out of the house and into an apartment in the next city. About three months after he moved into his new apartment, Earl started seeing Alice. Earl and Alice were dating for about six months, when Earl filed for divorce from my grandmother and moved in with Alice. It was a bitter divorce. Neither Earl nor my grandmother would budge on the property issues. Plus, I am sure my grandmother was not thrilled about Alice.

I think Earl and Alice had been living together for about five or six months when Earl had a heart attack. My grandmother, who was still married to Earl, was Earl's closest living relative. She relished the position—and the power.

My grandmother was at the hospital every day from early in the morning until late at night. Although I would like to think my grandmother was hoping Earl would pull through, she spent most of her energy ensuring that Alice kept as far away from Earl as possible. My grandmother gave strict instructions to the hospital staff that Alice was neither allowed to see Earl nor receive any information about his health status. Maybe she was just distraught over Earl's health condition, but when visiting hours were over she went out with friends and played bridge. I might even think that she blamed Alice for Earl's heart attack, because it occurred while he was with Alice, but Earl had had problems with his heart for years.

My real grandfather died before I was born. Earl married my grandmother when I was five. He was the only grandfather I ever knew. I think he felt especially close to me, too. Even after he and my grandmother separated, we got together for Sunday morning breakfasts. He seemed so content after he met Alice. It was the first time in a long time I had seen him so relaxed.

Earl was in intensive care for a week. When they moved him to a regular room, I was able to sit and visit with him. Well, it was mostly sitting with him, because he mostly floated in and out of consciousness. On two different occasions he called me Alice. I tried to talk my grandmother into letting Alice see Earl, but she was adamantly against it. She wasn't spending the time with him herself. She mostly sat in the waiting room with other relatives playing the role of grieving spouse.

Earl suffered a fatal heart attack in the hospital about three weeks after he was first admitted. He died without ever seeing Alice again.

Your Plan Doesn't Stop When Your Marriage Ends

When people are divorcing, there is so much focus on the division of assets and custody of the children that the parties often forget to revise their estate plans. With everything going on at that time, it is understandable that estate planning issues get lost in the shuffle. When you lose trust in your spouse and no longer want to spend your life with that person, why would you ever allow him or her to be in charge of your medical care? Earl had never been happier than when he moved in with Alice. Yet, his divorcing spouse made all of the decisions regarding his medical care. In the face of death, the property issues seem trivial compared to the personal issues. Earl would likely have rather died a pauper with Alice at his bedside than a wealthy man alone in the hospital.

With life events such as divorce or breakup, it is important to immediately make the changes needed to have the people you want in charge of making decisions about your life and your death.

JANET'S STORY

My partner and I had been together for 14 years when I received the worst phone call of my life. There had been a terrible accident, and she was being flown to the hospital by helicopter. The hospital staff wanted to know how to get in touch with her next of kin. Mine was the only phone number they could find in her wallet. I gave them her parents' phone number, got into the car and drove straight to the hospital.

When I arrived at the hospital, I couldn't get any information on Janet's condition. The hospital staff informed me that medical information could only be released to Janet's family. For them, family did not include live-in partners, regardless of the length of the relationship. It took six hours for Janet's parents to arrive at the hospital. During that time, I sat in the hospital waiting room and wasn't allowed to see or comfort her.

Only after Janet's parents arrived was I able to see her. Thankfully, they were caring people who accepted our relationship. The doctors predicted that Janet would not make it through the night. She died within the next hour. All that time had been wasted as I sat in that dark waiting room. She had been slowly dying alone, when I should have been holding her hand and couldn't.

There are several key situations that *require* having proper health care directives or similar types of documents:

- *When you have a strong relationship with someone who is not your spouse.* If you are living with a partner, whether the same or opposite sex, it is important to have documents that afford the person the same rights as a family member. Hospitals generally have hard and fast rules about who is a family member. Most of the time, unmarried partners are not considered family members. This was the case with Janet and her partner. As a result, Janet's last hours were spent alone until her parents arrived and gave their permission. This can be especially important where there is animosity between the family and the nonfamily partner. Today, many couples live together without ever getting married. Although they may think of themselves as a unit, without having documents to prove otherwise, parents who don't approve the relationship can come in and keep the partner from participating in medical decisions, and even prevent them from entering the hospital room.

- *When the person who is authorized under the law is not the person you want making your medical decisions for you.* In both Jack's father's case and Earl's case, their spouses were the people entitled to make all medical, burial, and other related decisions for them. It may be true that most people want their spouse to make these decisions, but it is not true for everyone. What if you have a situation like Jack's father or Earl, or you have a spouse who does not feel the same as you do about life support, organ donation, or any of the other decisions that may need to be made for you? If you are not married but have children, your children will often be the ones entitled by law to make these decisions for you. In most states, children age 18 are entitled to act on behalf of their parents, absent some other direction. These types of decisions are difficult to make for a loved one at any age, but imagine trying to make them at age 18. Without some word from you otherwise, your 18-year-old will be forced into that position. If you have no spouse and no children, typically the priority will be parents, followed by siblings. I once knew a woman who had been abused by her father as a child. As a result, she never married or had children. When she was dying, her closest living relative was her father. He made all of the arrangements regarding the disposition of her body. I guarantee that she would not have wanted her father to make those decisions for her.

- *When multiple people are entitled to make these decisions for you.* If your children have the highest priority and you have three children, all three of them have to agree on how to act. Most states have a unanimity rule with respect to making medical decisions. This means that if all three do not agree, those in favor of maintaining the status quo prevail. For example, if two children want life support discontinued and one child wants it to continue, the one who wants life support to continue will prevail, because that maintains the current status. That may be acceptable when it comes to decisions that require a "yes" or "no" answer but it will not work where actual choices need to be made. The best example would be the decision to bury or cremate. There is no status quo to maintain in this situation. The decision needs to be made to do one or the other. Depending on the state, it is possible that authorities will do nothing with your body until your children can finally agree.

KAREN'S LETTER

Dear Mom,

I am so sorry. I know you always said that you wanted to donate your organs for medical research. With three brothers and both parents having died from heart disease, I know you thought it was important to have someone study your body in the hope it could prevent others from dying too young. I remember when Uncle Joe died last fall, we spent hours talking about how great it would be to see a medical breakthrough in this area. You told me you were impressed that Uncle Joe had made arrangements to donate his organs for medical research and were surprised that it upset his family so much. It seemed clear to me that you wished to do the same.

Apparently, you were not so clear with Colin and Anna. When I got to the hospital, they were already there. The doctors told us the stroke had left you with no brain activity and recommended we remove life support. It was the hardest thing we ever had to do. I told the doctors you wanted to donate your organs for medical research and asked about the procedure. I was shocked at how quickly and aggressively Colin and Anna objected. Neither of them wanted you to be "cut up." I tried to calmly explain that these were your wishes. They didn't believe me. They told me you had never mentioned such a thing to either of them. They accused me of trying to impose my desires on the situation.

Because you did not make your wishes known to them and did not designate one of us to speak in your place, we were required to make a unanimous decision. Without the agreement of all three of us, the hospital would do nothing. I argued, cajoled, and begged, but there was no convincing Colin and Anna.

A couple of weeks after your funeral, I read in the newspaper that the local university hospital was conducting new research on heart disease. I know you would have wanted your organs to be used in the research.

Love,

Karen

Only You Can Make Your Wishes Clear

Karen's mother felt strongly about the need to donate organs for medical research, yet she failed to make those wishes known to the people who had the power to make it happen—her children. Without a consensus, a hospital is going to take the path of least resistance and do nothing. Even though it sounds as if Uncle Joe's family had much the same reaction as Colin and Anna, he had taken the steps necessary before his death, and his wishes were carried out. When your desires may not reflect those of the ones who may have to make decisions for you, the best thing to do is to put them in writing. Otherwise, your desires may not be carried out.

Estate planning really isn't about the money as much as it is about communication—about telling your loved ones what is important to you. The money is just the means by which you can impart to your loved ones important life lessons. However, the lessons may never be learned, if you do not communicate them in a way that your loved ones can receive them.

MARY'S STORY

My mother married my stepfather when I was small. He had three children from a prior marriage, but they lived with their mother in another town. My stepfather and I were always close. He and my mother had not been married long before I began to think of him as my father. After he and my mother had been married for several years, he adopted me. I felt like I had truly become his daughter.

As my parents got older, I took on the responsibility of taking care of them. My stepbrothers and stepsister visited from time to time, but I felt as if I were the only one there for my parents. My mother got very sick a few years ago, and I devoted full-time working hours to care for her, and Dad, too. My mother had only been dead about six months when my father became sick. I was glad to have the opportunity to spend his last months together with him. Although I always felt we had a close relationship, we became even closer during those last few months.

I was the named trustee of my father's trust. It was a very straightforward trust—everything was split equally four ways. Even though I spent a great deal of time caring for my parents at the end of their lives, I felt this was a fair division of the estate. Besides the estate assets, there were a few accounts that had been in both my parents' names, which my father changed to his and my names after my mother died. It was my intention to divide the money from those accounts four ways as well, after I paid the hospital expenses.

Although I knew about the joint bank accounts, I didn't know that my father had named me as the sole beneficiary on his IRA. I have thought long and hard about whether to split that account four ways. As time goes on, however, I am beginning to think that I may just keep the IRA myself. After all, my father must have meant for me to have it if he made me the only beneficiary. Plus, my stepsiblings have been just awful since Dad died. They expect me to get everything organized, appraised, and sold immediately, so they can receive their share of the money. It's all about the money for them. They were not the least bit emotional when I sold Dad's house. I cried for three days.

For now, I think I will keep the IRA money a secret, at least until I decide what I am going to do with it. After all, I am the named beneficiary, and there is nothing that says I have to give them the money.

JEAN'S STORY

I guess I have always been jealous of Mary's relationship with my father. Although we lived with my mother an hour away, Mary got to see Dad every day. A couple of years after he married Mary's mother, my father adopted Mary. Being a young girl, I felt that he picked her over me. It is funny looking back, because even as he was adopting Mary, he still did plenty of things to show us he loved us all equally.

As I got older, life got more complicated, and it was difficult to always see my father and stepmother. When Dad got sick, I tried to be there for him. I offered on plenty of occasions to drive him to the doctor or pick up things for him from the store. However, Mary was always there, saying that she had things handled. I feel bad that I didn't take the chance to show my father what kind of daughter I could be.

Since Dad's death, Mary has still been running the show. I was not surprised to find out she was the successor trustee of Dad's trust. She was the one driving him to the lawyer's office, so why would he have chosen any of us? But, just like my dad, he still named the four of us as equal beneficiaries of his trust.

I recently discovered through my stockbroker (Dad and I used the same stockbroker) that Dad named Mary as the sole beneficiary of his IRA. Mary has not said one word about Dad's IRA since his death. My initial reaction was that Mary had somehow coerced Dad into changing the beneficiary to only her. She was, after all, driving him to and from the lawyer, the accountant, the doctor, the banker, and the broker all of the time. Dad was a strong man, and I just could not imagine him giving in to any kind of coercion. Then it hit me. My father was not trying to name Mary as the sole beneficiary. He named Mary because she was the successor trustee of his trust and would be able to distribute the IRA among all four of us.

I am not sure how much longer I am going to wait for Mary to tell us about the IRA. If it is not soon, I will be forced to take matters into my own hands.

The Key to Success Is Communication

If Mary and Jean's father had just communicated to them his intention in leaving the IRA to Mary, there would be no confusion. Instead, Mary thinks he left it to her, because she cared for her parents when they were ill, and Jean thinks her dad left it to Mary as trustee to distribute among all four children. He could have put a provision in his trust indicating that any retirement plans passing outside of the trust were intended to pass directly to the named beneficiaries. Jean might still be inclined to think that Mary actually coerced him into the distribution. Again, if he simply communicated that Mary was receiving the extra assets because of the time she had spent with him and his wife, that would have cleared up any confusion.

Oftentimes, the easiest way to avoid future problems is to explain why you are doing something. If you are leaving more to one child than another, then explain why. You may not convince the child who is receiving the smaller amount as to your wisdom, but you may be able to avoid additional problems between the two children as a result. The more explanation from you, the less likely there will be disagreements between your heirs after you are gone.

Put some of you and some of your thoughts into your estate plan. If you struggled over some issue in your plan, tell your family about the struggle. It may put things into perspective for them. Remember Scott and Gina in Chapter 7? Their mother had to decide how to divide her estate among her grandchildren in the event that Scott and Gina died. Gina did not know that her mother labored over this decision and had called the lawyer every day for a week to ask whether she had made the right choice. Gina also never thought about how it might be viewed by Scott if her mother had taken the other route. If Scott and Gina's mother had explained in her trust that she thought her solution would let the grandchildren know she loved each of them equally and how she thought each child would feel if she split the trust differently, maybe Gina wouldn't have been so angry.

When I go on a trip, I always write letters to my daughters telling them how much I care for them. I tell them how I see them today and what I hope for them in the future. I also tell them about my life and what stories about me I think they should know. If for some reason I cannot be here to tell them when they are 20, 30, or 40 what dreams I held for them when they were young, I can tell them anyway in my estate plan. I save all of my letters, and I put them with my estate plan. When the time comes for them to read my plan and they see the choices I have made for them, they will understand why I made the decisions I did. I don't want them to be left guessing. I also want their guardians and trustees to read the letters, so they can approach decisions regarding my children with my words in their minds and in their hearts.

I don't expect this to change as my children get older. As I get older, I still look to my parents for approval and affirmation. I still hope to learn from them and pass on the lessons I learn from them to my children and my grandchildren. What better way to receive those lessons than through heartfelt messages they leave me. I know if my parents choose to leave me less than one of my siblings, they will tell me the reasons why. They won't leave me guessing as to whether this was just a way of evening out the disparity in wealth among us or because I did something to offend them before they died. Or, if they decide to have distributions conditioned on employment status, I hope they will share with me their experiences living through the Depression and how that experience instilled in them the importance of a strong work ethic. Otherwise, I may just see their conditions and restrictions as a means of controlling me, and I will not learn the lesson they are trying to share.

No matter how much or how little money is involved, by communicating your ideas and intentions to your loved ones, you can ensure your best intentions are carried out. Remember that your lessons are only as good as the mechanism by which you communicate them. This book has been devoted to telling you the stories of those who have gone before. They had the best of intentions but failed to adequately communicate the wisdom they had to share. Learn from their mistakes. Take your best intentions and let them be realized.

EPILOGUE

When we first decided to write this book, our concept was to focus on the emotional rather than financial aspects of estate planning. We thought it was time to address this dimension of estate planning in such a way that would enable people to discover what was important to them in their life experiences and pass these on to their loved ones. We wanted to share ways to pass more than just financial wealth at death.

As we started to talk about these ideas with our clients and friends, they told us their stories. The stories of families and friends who failed to realize their best intentions were compelling. We realized there were lessons in every story we heard. Life lessons they tried to teach their loved ones may not have been appreciated by their families, but that does not mean their attempts to pass on these messages were in vain. We thought by sharing their stories you might be inspired to design a plan that would live up to your best intentions.

We hope you will learn from the people whose stories we have told. There is something each of us can take from virtually every story. We hope you will take the messages from these stories and apply them to your own family and estate planning. In the end, we hope you will enable your loved ones to actually fulfill their best intentions.

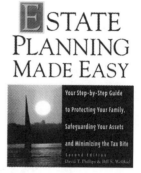

Best Intentions

For special discounts on 20 or more copies of *Best Intentions: Ensuring Your Estate Plan Delivers Both Wealth and Wisdom,* please call Dearborn Trade Special Sales at 800-621-9621, extension 4455.

Dearborn™
Trade Publishing
A **Kaplan Professional** Company